GENERATIONAL
IMPACT

JEFFREY A. KLICK. PH.D.

GENERATIONAL
IMPACT

A VISION FOR
THE FAMILY

TATE PUBLISHING & *Enterprises*

Published by Tate Publishing & Enterprises, LLC
127 E. Trade Center Terrace | Mustang, Oklahoma 73064 USA
1.888.361.9473 | www.tatepublishing.com

Tate Publishing is committed to excellence in the publishing industry. The company reflects the philosophy established by the founders, based on Psalm 68:11,
"The Lord gave the word and great was the company of those who published it."

Book design copyright © 2010 by Tate Publishing, LLC. All rights reserved.
Cover design by Lauran Levy
Interior design by Blake Brasor

Published in the United States of America

ISBN: 978-1-61739-536-9
1. Family & Relationships / Parenting / General
2. Religion / Christian Life / Family
10.10.20

DEDICATION

This book is dedicated to the most wonderful family God ever gave to a man:

To the wife of my youth, who has helped me become who I am and whom I love more today than when we first met.

To Andrea, Sarah, and David, my arrows, and to my sons-in-law, Brian and Jeffrey—I thank God daily for each of you!

To Lydia, Katelyn, Mackenzie, Daniel, Nathan, Alexis, Treya, Havilah, and Addie, the best grandchildren in the world!

Thank you all for loving me and helping me to grow up in Christ.

ACKNOWLEDGMENTS

A very special thank you is due to Angelina Liu, Amy Hall, and Hannah with Tate Publishing for their editing and comments. I greatly appreciate your time and labor of love to assist me in completing this book. May the LORD bless you as much as you have me for your generous time investment in this work. Also, a big thank you to the wonderful people of Hope Family Fellowship who love and support me on a daily basis!

The Purpose of This Book

As I was sitting in the hospital room holding our fifth granddaughter, the revelation hit me that I was no longer a young man. I know it should have dawned on me sooner, but I was too busy to dwell on such things. Having turned fifty-four recently (and now with four additional grandchildren), my thoughts yet again turn to those who will follow in my steps when I leave this earth for my reward. What am I leaving them? How will I be remembered?

This book is an effort to leave something behind that might help those who are in my wake. What is presented is not a list of dos and don'ts or a "how to succeed in three easy steps" type program but rather an overarching philosophy for the family. Our philosophical understanding will ultimately direct our actions. I pray that the viewpoint presented in this book will help you, produce fruit that will last, and bring glory to our wonderful LORD Jesus.

TABLE OF CONTENTS

Introduction 13

No Greater Joy (or Pain) 19

A Divine Blueprint. 25

Understanding Biblical Authority 35

Generational Warfare. 51

United We Stand 59

God, Did You Make a Mistake?. 69

Children Are a Blessing—Really, They Are! 77

All Parents Train 85

Dr. Spock Was Not a Theologian. 93

God Loves Discipline. 103

Behavior Issues Other Than Rebellion. 113

Five Key Concepts 119

Common Parental Questions. 137

Dating or Courtship. 151

What about the Church? 159

A Note to Grandparents
       (Including Future Ones!). 173

Some Final Thoughts. 179

Appendix 183

INTRODUCTION

And there arose another generation after them who did not
know the LORD or the work that He had done for Israel.

Judges 2:10

I firmly believe in missions, evangelism, and the ministry of the
church. Maybe you are thinking, *That is a strange way to start a book
about God's plan for reaching the next generation.* Actually, I want
to make sure there is no confusion from the beginning regarding
what I believe, because there is always someone who will say I'm
too "home" focused and not enough "lost" focused. There is that
danger when you emphasize one side of an argument, but in spite
of the risk, I remain convinced that one of God's greatest tools for
reaching the lost is a godly family. As our society continues to spiral
into darkness, a family that functions in a loving, biblical manner
will shine even brighter.

A casual reading through the Old Testament will reveal what
is meant by "generational impact." It has often struck me as I've
read through Samuel, Kings, and Chronicles that one king or ruler
would arise and do great exploits for God and then his son would be
a dismal failure. Almost every reform that was accomplished in the
godly ruler's lifetime was undone in the next generation. Here is a
sampling of what I mean: Eli was a man of God, but his sons were
thieves and also immoral. Samuel was one of the greatest prophets who spoke for God, ruled Israel, and anointed two kings, yet
his sons were corrupt, wicked men. Solomon produced Rehoboam,
Jehoshaphat produced Jehoram, Hezekiah produced Manasseh,
and Josiah produced Jehoahaz. Solomon, Jehoshaphat, Hezekiah,

and Josiah were major reformers who brought godly revivals to their nation, yet their children were wicked and destroyed everything that their fathers had accomplished. All of the good works were effectively lost within one generation. The righteous reforms made by the godly were undone by the next generation. Somehow, these godly men, who had changed their nation, had not captured their children's hearts for the Lord. How easy it seems for evil to be transferred to the next generation, and how difficult for righteousness to continue. Perhaps because it is so natural to be wicked and so supernatural to not be. How do we fail to impart to the generation following us the passion that drives us? How could a generation not know the Lord after all God had done for them in the verses above? What were the parents doing, or perhaps better stated, not doing?

Studies show a mass exodus of young people from the faith of their parents by the time they reach the first year of college—averaging somewhere between 70 and 90 percent! How can this be? Most of these young people have been raised in Christian homes. They have been given the best training in Sunday school, nurseries, children's ministries, youth groups, and Christian schools, yet alarming numbers are leaving the faith. Something is wrong, and drastic changes are necessary to avoid disaster. The water temperature is rising, and the frog just sits in the pot relaxing. It is time to jump from the kettle!

The purpose of this book is to challenge parents to capture the next generation for Christ. If we reach the whole world in our generation but fail to capture our own children's hearts, we may lose all we gained. My desire is to see many godly generations loving and serving the Lord. I want to be the great-great-great-grandfather who started a revival that has influenced generations. I believe that is your heart also or you would not be reading a book like this. The task is before us, and future generations are at risk. Please read the following chapters with an open mind. The thoughts and views expressed here are not "normal," but I firmly believe they are biblical. I hope your heart's desire is like mine. I never wanted "normal" children; I wanted godly children, and there is a vast difference between the two.

One note as we begin. As the date of this writing, our three children are all over thirty years old. My wife and I have been married more than thirty-five years and we have nine grandchildren. I have often stated, "In order to be disillusioned, we must first have an illusion." When we began this journey of being parents, we had an illusion. We believed that if we trained our children, controlled their education, limited their friendships and outside experiences that we would have almost perfect children when they reached adulthood. We read many books and listened to several speakers who boldly proclaimed that if we just followed their advice, all would be well. By the way, most of the writers and speakers had young children and really had not walked through much of life yet, but that, of course, is a different story!

What we discovered is that when our children grew in age, they were not perfect. Each one faced temptations, struggles, and battles just like every other human that has lived before them. As they entered marriage and began careers, started having children and walking through life, failures came. Perfection was not achieved, and we often wondered why not. Where had we failed? We had followed the books, invested our lives, and attempted to give our children everything of value. Why had things not always worked out the way we thought it would? The truth we have to understand is that all children will become adults, and on the way, they will have their own struggles with their flesh and sinful nature.

> Each child will face battles and experience victory and defeat, just as you and I do.

Our job as parents is to help prepare them for this war called "life." We cannot live it for them, but we train them, pray for them, love them, and support them as they walk through each conflict. Children will have their own walk with God, and each one will mature at a different rate. Some of the values that you have as a parent your children may not embrace when they are grown. Most parents are at least twenty years older and often possess thirty or more years' life experience than their children. Our understanding has changed considerably over this period, and so will your children's. As they grow older, views will change, and the training you invested in them will return. The value systems you attempted to put into them will produce fruit.

We must realize that we can perform proper training and we can invest our lives in our children (and I believe we should!), but each child will still eventually have to possess his own walk with God. Children have the potential to sin, fall, and choose against their training. You might ask, "If this is the case, why bother?" God demands it of us, is the answer! We are stewards of the most precious resource on earth, children. We should do our very best and then trust the LORD to direct and keep His own. We cannot simply shrug our shoulders and say, "It doesn't matter." Of course it does! We are given the task, and we must do the best job possible. God loves our children, and He will see to it that He does not lose any of His own. Even if they struggle, which I guarantee they will, our God is bigger, and He has a wonderful plan for each one of them. Our job is to train, love, encourage, and constantly lift them up in prayer. God is the One who will do the saving and keeping!

The point is we do our best and leave the rest in God's hands. Our adult children will face difficulties, and they will struggle, but just like us, God loves them, and He is working in their lives. Do not lose heart and do not quit. Our God is faithful!

> Train up a child in the way he should go; even when he is old he will not depart from it.
>
> Proverbs 22:6

We often read this passage in one of two ways. We either read it as a release from our responsibility for training, because after all, God will make sure the child returns after he rebels at some time in the future. Alternatively, we read it as a guarantee that our children will never struggle or fail. Both readings are incorrect. Proverbs are not a guarantee of anything but simply words of wisdom to live by. For example one Proverb states that "gray hair is a sign of wisdom" (Proverbs 16:31), but we all know people with gray hair who are unwise. Proverbs are sagely phrases full of principles and wisdom, not absolute promises or the entire truth on any particular topic. Confusing this can lead to frustration and disillusionment.

In the verse above, we are instructed to train our children in the way that is right, and we are told that when he is old he will not depart from it. What is not written there is that the child may reject it, question it, reprocess it, repackage it, and yes, even keep it. If we do a good job of training he cannot depart from it for the training will always be in his heart and mind. We are commanded to do the training; God is the one who will keep it current in the hearts and minds of our children. Our children may fail and choose foolishly, but they will be choosing *against* what they know is right, instead of just blindly stumbling along as many of us did.

As we have looked back over the years, we see things we could have done differently, for hindsight is always clearer than what we currently see. In addition, our adult children have shared with us some of the ways in which we failed them as they were growing up. No parent is perfect, and we were far from it. One truth we have grasped is that we did the best we knew how, and we would not change any of the underlying philosophical understandings that we held. Many of those views will be presented in the following pages for your prayerful consideration. There are no perfect parents, only a perfect Savior. As imperfect parents, we attempt to do the best we can, and I pray that this book will assist you in your pursuit of making a generational impact.

A philosophical mind-set firmly rooted in the Scripture, rather than a point-by-point handbook, is presented within these pages. Each child and every family is a one-of-a-kind experience. Therefore, our daily dependence on God demands that we work in more general principles and not legalistic steps. A "one size fits all" mentality does not work. Every family has their own path to walk, and there is plenty of room for the God-given individual expression each of us possess. God has placed each member of the family in the exact place that He desired to help accomplish His purposes. God does not make mistakes. God put your family together in just the way He intended, and He has a perfect plan that He is implementing.

The first section of the book will present a biblical examination of the roles of each member of the family. After we examine these, then the application will be presented as we attempt to raise our children for the glory of God.

Please pause a moment and ask God to give you "ears to hear what He would say to you" as you read the rest of this book. If you encounter ideas that you cannot accept right now, do not throw the book across the room but shelve the idea until another time. Perhaps it will grow on you. Implement what you can and pray over the rest. Just because a concept or idea is different does not necessarily mean it is wrong. It just may be different. What I am sharing in this book has been tried and tested by years of experience. Both failures and successes are included. My prayer is that you will be able to profit from both.

No Greater Joy (or Pain)

And I declare to him that I am about to punish his house forever, for the iniquity that he knew because his sons were blaspheming God, and he did not restrain them.

1 Samuel 3:13

Why are so many young people from Christian homes backsliding? Why does almost every church youth group in America pray for revival? Why are PKs (preachers' kids) and MKs (missionary kids) often the worst children in the church and the subject of so many jokes? Why is the divorce rate among Christians the same as non-Christians? Why are so many Christian young people getting pregnant before they are married? Why are we spending countless dollars to reach the lost but losing our children right under our own roof? Why will we spend multiple evenings away from home and invest millions of dollars on discipleship programs yet not disciple those who live with us? These questions often fill my mind. Could it be that the church at large has missed some of the basic commands about training the next generation? Could it be that we are already reaping some of the fruit of our failure to train the next generation? Sadly, I believe so.

Churches often allocate large portions of their budgets for missions, youth work, children's ministries, and a host of other programs, but what part of the budget goes to actually training parents to capture the next generation? Some groups will teach a child-training class or two or even host a marriage seminar. While helpful, these are hardly enough. This lack of training reminds me of parking an ambulance at the bottom of a cliff, waiting to attend to the wounded that have gone over the edge. Of course this is necessary, but the question has to be asked: Why can't we help them not go over that cliff in the first place? Why not build a rail at the top of the cliff and help keep people from crashing through the rail? Why do we focus so much on recovery programs and so little on prevention programs? Many of the weekly programs that the church offers are trying to make up for what should be taking place daily in the home. Many good-intentioned parents delegate the responsibility of training their children to a church staff member or school teacher, believing that the professionals are more qualified. By this transference of duty, the parent sometimes feels that they have fulfilled their task, but I believe this is very shortsighted.

There is a huge price to pay for parental failure in training the next generation, and many studies point to the fact that the church is already paying it. On the other hand, there is a wonderful reward for those that invest the energy required to train the next generation. There is joy in having grown children who are walking with God, and it is unlike any other feeling possible. John the beloved stated it this way:

> I have no greater joy than to hear that my children are walking in the truth.
>
> 3 John 4

I know this verse is probably referring to spiritual children, but having your grown children love the LORD and desire with all their hearts to serve God will give a great joy unlike any other a person can experience. Knowing that the labor has paid off and all the time and effort is producing a crop of godliness is worth any price that was paid. As our children age and our relationship moves into an even better place, we continue to reap a harvest of peace and joy. Of course there are trials and disappointments in every family, but having a wonderful relationship with your adult children is priceless. The goal of having adult children who walk with God should always be in front of us as we live each day. Why are we doing all that we do as parents if that is not the goal?

As a pastor for many years, I have seen the despairing side of parenting all too often. If no greater joy is obtained by seeing our children walk in the truth, the other side is also true. No greater heartache is experienced than to see our children walk in sin, error, and rebellion. Crying with parents whose children have rejected Christ, the Bible, and their parents' faith gives a unique insight into the pain only known by these parents. The reality of knowing that your children are not walking with God is a heavy burden that parents carry and many times leads to a lifetime of regret. The pleasure received from the things that squeezed out and replaced the parental duty now pale in comparison to the pain experienced. Short-term pleasure rarely replaces long-term heartache in such choices. The temporary happiness experienced from many of the activities, recreations, and diversions that stole our precious time now fades in comparison to the emotional trauma being endured.

There is an enormous price to pay for failing to capture our child's heart. This price includes emotional heartache, frustration over adult children that are immature, and the pain of watching these new parents pass on to their children the same errors that we may have given to them. We grieve as we watch the cycle repeat itself in the next generation with multiple divorces, abuse, workaholics, lack of interest in the work of God and His church. It does not have to be this way! Given this backdrop, my conviction is steeled; reaching our children is of primary importance in keeping the fruit of our labors in serving our LORD. God has called us to make disciples, and the first ones gained should be those of our own household. If we fail to capture those disciples *in* our home, we will not be comforted much by those we make *outside* of the home. If Christianity has not been effective in the home, please do not export it somewhere else until it becomes so!

We do not have to look very far to see that the generation following our example is in deep trouble. Just about every type of crime imaginable is being committed in our society, and this is especially true among young people. The value system around us is completely upside down. A child needs a parent's permission to be given an aspirin at the government schools, but abortions can be had without notice. A walk through just about any mall or teen hangout will reveal what is important to this culture. Booming music full of sexually explicit terms, profanities and extreme violence is quite the rage leading to a hard-hearted youth culture.

In addition, as discouraging as this may be in our society, the church at large is not very much different. While the believers may not be as bad as the world around them, they are not far behind. Recent studies by the Barna Research Group (and others) indicates that the investment of resources that the church is making into the youth is paying little dividends when this group reaches twenty. The vast majority of young people end up rejecting their training and choosing to walk away from the church. Something must be done, and soon, or yet another generation will slip into imitating the world system instead of trying to engage it for Christ. A friend of mine has aptly stated, "The world has done a far better job of evangelizing the church than the church has the world."

Those that do not know Christ observe our families, and they are waiting for a difference to be shown. The family is the place for that difference to be birthed, nurtured, and then exported to a very needy world. The church has tried the world's system for parenting, and the last twenty to thirty years have produced some of the laziest, selfish, most self-centered people around. Many employers are hard pressed to find an employee who will give a full day's labor for a full day's pay. Often employers complain of the difficulty of finding someone who has character or ambition. The young people trained under the world's philosophy are entertainment oriented and very good at complaining, but self-sacrifice, honor, diligence, honesty, and creativity are severely lacking. Unlike their ancestors, who learned to live through wars, a depression, and financial insecurity, this generation has yet to be severely challenged. Since the 1960s free love and self-satisfaction has ruled instead of selflessness and fidelity. What is to be the norm in the next generation will depend largely on how this generation accepts the challenge of training their children. Will we return to discipline and self-sacrifice, or will we continue with the feel-good anything-goes mind-set? I believe that those who accept the challenge to train their children will help propel them into leadership roles in the future. The world around us is crying out for someone who has firm standards and knows how to act when all is shaking. May we seek the baton that was dropped by the last generation, pick it up, and hand it on to the next!

QUESTIONS TO PRAY ABOUT

Have I thought about the questions at the beginning of this chapter?

Have I invested in others but neglected my own family?

Are those under my roof genuine believers and growing disciples?

Am I willing to invest whatever is necessary to experience that "no greater joy" of which John spoke?

Am I imitating the world in how I dress, act, think, entertain myself, and relate to others?

> "Children who are raised in godly homes and from their earliest days are trained in the faith find their later church experience all the more meaningful. Christian parents, not church pastors and teachers, have the primary responsibly. All in all, the home must be the primary center of Christian nurture and teaching."
>
> —J. Rodman Williams, *Renewal Theology*

A Divine Blueprint

But as it is, God arranged the members in the body,
each one of them, as He chose.

1 Corinthians 12:18

God has given specific commands to each member of the family. For the last few generations the world system around us has attempted to blur the distinctions, but Scripture does not lack clarity on the issue. The Bible presents very clear guidance for men, women, and children as to their roles in the family structure. An understanding of these individual roles will help shape our philosophic approach to the family. Throughout the book, I will be sharing more on the role of each member of the family, but I wanted to present a general introduction here to get us all on the same page (pun intended).

First, God clearly places the responsibility of leading the family on the man's shoulders.

But I want you to understand that the head of every man is Christ, the head of a wife is her husband, and the head of Christ is God.

1 Corinthians 11:3

Wives, submit to your own husbands, as to the Lord. For the husband is the head of the wife even as Christ is the head of the church, his body, and is himself its Savior. Now as the church submits to Christ, so also wives should submit in everything to their husbands.

Ephesians 5:22–24

The husband carries the responsibility to be the head of his wife and family. Headship includes having an understanding of leading, protecting, and exercising authority. Though many biblically illiterate men are familiar with the above passages of Scripture, most men will readily accept the authority part but often flinch when it comes to actually leading and protecting.

Even though many men have a clear understanding of the headship part, they often do not have quite as complete knowledge of their responsibility. Jesus makes it abundantly clear that true, biblical leadership begins with taking a servant position.

> But Jesus called them to him and said, "You know that the rulers of the Gentiles lord it over them, and their great ones exercise authority over them. It shall not be so among you. But whoever would be great among you must be your servant."
>
> Matthew 20:25–26

This command is true for fathers and husbands as well as the apostles to whom Jesus was speaking. Respect is earned, not demanded, and so is the ability to have followers, including a wife and children. Husbands and fathers have been placed in a position of authority by God; therefore, they bear the weight of the responsibility. However, those under their care can choose to follow or reject them based on how the leader leads.

A paraphrased thought from Ken Nair's challenging book *Discovering the Mind of a Woman* goes something like this: "As the leader of your home, how are those under your leadership doing? If you have been married five, ten, or fifteen years, is your wife better or worse by being under your leadership?" The same question from Nair can be asked about the children under the father's care. Are they better or worse after being under your leadership? This is a scary thought to ponder!

Another passage to consider further is

> Likewise, husbands, live with your wives in an understanding way, showing honor to the woman as the weaker vessel, since

> they are heirs with you of the grace of life, so that your prayers
> may not be hindered.
>
> 1 Peter 3:7

The husband is specifically challenged to live with his wife in an understanding way, which places the responsibility on the man. Part of this understanding must be in attempting to grasp what the wife needs, how she thinks, what her dreams and visions are for the family, and a host of other thoughts. Peter even states that the prayers of the man can be hindered if he does not live in this fashion.

I mentioned that men struggle with understanding that protection is more than simply chasing away an intruder that might be in the home. Wives need to know that their "head" will protect them emotionally and spiritually as well as physically. A man that simply states, "I bring home a paycheck. What more does she want?" does not grasp that his wife needs a great deal more than money. The wife needs her husband's protection from an intrusive mother-in-law, other demanding women, even the children when they challenge her position. The wife must know that the husband will provide her shelter that far exceeds simple material provision. The wife needs the security of knowing that she is the most important person in her husband's life, next to the LORD. The wife needs to *know* (by constant reinforcement) that the husband will always choose her above his mother, his job, his ministry, any other woman, and even the children. An insecure wife often develops into a contentious one.

The biblical type of leadership in the Ephesians passage is very different than that exercised in our society. Paul gives us the example to follow, and it is very challenging if we stop to think about it.

> Husbands, love your wives, as Christ loved the church and gave
> himself up for her.
>
> Ephesians 5:25a

Christ loved the church perfectly. He selflessly gave up His life for her. Mortal man will not be perfect, but we *can* lay down our lives daily for our wife and children, which is required in the exercising of our headship. God expects the man to be a servant leader who dies to himself daily for those under his care.

What does "dying to yourself" look like? It depends on the day! Christ did not demand His own way but in perfect humility followed His Father's voice. As earthly husbands and fathers, we also must have a personal relationship with our heavenly Father. We must be men that actively seek His will and study His Word. As we seek God's will, many cloudy issues become clearer. The demand for self-fulfillment and gratification diminishes. Always having to win every argument and protect our reputation or position gives way to service and esteeming others as better than ourselves. (See Philippians 2:3.) Our families have little trouble following our lead if we are trying to walk as servants.

In practice, dying to ourselves means that we simply let go of many insignificant issues. There are some issues worth fighting for and standing our ground on, and many others that really don't matter all that much. If I esteem my wife and value her, I will seek her input in all major decisions and even the minor ones that directly affect her. Making choices for her while not allowing her input communicates that I simply don't value her or desire to listen to her. This is not walking in Christ's love!

I will touch on the role of the husband and father more, but for now, we need to learn how to seek the LORD daily, talk, communicate, serve, die to our selves, and love our wives in order to be a good head.

THE ROLE OF THE WOMAN:

The wife is given as a helpmeet (Genesis 2:18) to her husband, and a significant part of what she does is assist and respect him. Men need respect to have the courage to lead, and primarily this will come from the wife. If this need is not met at home, the man will find it somewhere else, such as in work, friends, or sports.

The wisest of women builds her house, but folly with her own hands tears it down.

Proverbs 14:1

What a wife says to her husband can produce life or death, build him up or tear him down, help him be a leader or neuter him spiritually.

Many women have shared that they wish their husbands would pray with them. In a follow-up question, they are asked if they ever prayed as a couple at any time in their lives. Usually they will reply that they *used* to pray but then they stopped. What the woman does not understand is that in my counseling with hundreds of men, it is clear *why* they stopped praying with their wives. What men will typically relate is that they used to pray with their wife and children, but then the wife made a comment, something like, "You call *that* a prayer?" or "Is that it? That's *all* we are going to pray about." While those questions may seem within the boundaries of reason, what the wife does not realize is that the man just felt slapped, and it will take a while before he attempts to lead again. Not too many men like to be put down or made fun of in this arena, especially in front of the children. Men will take this attack as a lack of respect, and the typical response is to lock down spiritually. A wise woman will build her home by thanking her husband and encouraging any prayer, no matter how trivial it may seem to her at the time. Like priming a pump, if the man feels safe in praying, he will pray more and will develop "better" prayers as time passes. Personal observation and interaction with many couples has confirmed that the wife's respect of her husband will typically unlock more mature behavior in the husband.

While not necessarily politically correct in our day, the following is biblically accurate. The wife is told repeatedly in Ephesians 5 to submit to her husband. Submit does not mean to be a doormat in the original Greek language that the New Testament uses but instead to willingly line up under an authority.

Wives, submit to your own husbands, as to the LORD. For the husband is the head of the wife even as Christ is the head of the church, his body, and is himself its Savior. Now as the church

submits to Christ, so also wives should submit in everything to
their husbands.

Ephesians 5:22–24

As a wife willingly lines up under (submits to) her husband, she is
demonstrating great faith to her children. The story of the Roman
centurion in Matthew 8:5–9 clearly knits together faith and authority. A soldier approaches Jesus with a request for healing, and Jesus
graciously agrees to follow him. The soldier states that Jesus does
not need to come, just simply say the word, and his servant will be
healed. The centurion's rationale is what is interesting in this story.
"I too am a man under authority and I say to this one come, and he
comes, and to another go, and he goes." This Roman clearly understood authority. Jesus makes a fascinating comment after the centurion leaves. "I have not seen such great faith in all of Israel." It would
seem logical for Jesus to have said, "I have not seen such a great
understanding of authority in all of Israel," but He did not say that.
Jesus linked an understanding of being under authority with great
faith. It is not a stretch to state that a wife who willingly lines up
under her husband's authority must possess faith in order to believe
that God will protect her, provide for her, lead her, and bless her, for
following an imperfect man.

As the wife demonstrates this process to her children, she is training them for their future responsibility as well. Young sons are learning how a godly wife follows her husband and therefore discovering
that he needs to use his authority wisely if he marries. Daughters are
being given an example of how to follow their future husband's leadership. This training is being given, regardless of whether the wife
is performing her task well or poorly, for modeling is always taking
place. The children are observing the behavior of their mother, and
they will emulate her when they begin their own family.

Paul's summary of the passage in Ephesians 5 perfectly captures
both of the responsibilities of the husband and wife.

> However, let each one of you love his wife as himself, and let the
> wife see that she respects her husband.
>
> Ephesians 5:33

A husband must love his wife, and a wife must see that she respects her husband. A man desperately needs to be respected by his wife and children as much as the wife needs to be loved and protected. A foolish wife will tear down her husband and then wonder why he has no backbone. She ridicules his leadership skills and then criticizes his lack of leading. A foolish wife will expose her husband's weakness in public and then not be able to figure out why her husband does not trust in her.

From personal experience, I can tell you that the best thing my wife did for me as a young man was to find something to respect in me. As to what that was, you will have to ask her, but I know she supported me in the good times and bad. My wife never has shared my failures with others and always demanded that the children respect me as their father. I did not have to worry about her talking to other women about me or running me down to her folks. My wonderful wife protected my reputation. If she ever had a problem with me, she talked to me about it, and for that I am very grateful. If no one else respected me, she did, and it made a major difference in my life! Her respect gave me the confidence and security to grow up and lead my family.

THE ROLE OF CHILDREN:

Husbands are commanded by God to lead, wives demonstrate great faith by following their leadership, and both are teaching their children by their examples whether good or bad. The Scripture specifically commands children to obey their parents, and this action takes faith, humility, and submission on their part.

> Children, obey your parents in the LORD, for this is right.
>
> Ephesians 6:1

Children are to obey their parents, and God calls this "right." The word is actually translated as righteous in many translations, and it would seem to be the correct interpretation.

> Children, obey your parents in everything, for this pleases the LORD.
>
> Colossians 3:20

Everything is an all-inclusive word. As long as children are living under their parents' authority, they are to be obedient in all ways at all times. Of course, this does not mean that the child is to perform sinful acts, violate other Scriptures, or remain in a situation of abuse (the same is true for a wife). However, in the normal course of a Christian home, with dad and mom attempting to follow God, children have one primary responsibility—to obey. Even in homes where one or both of the parents are not Christians, the child can continue to learn many lessons if their heart remains submissive and open to God's instruction. God does not qualify the statement in either of the above verses limiting obedience to only godly parents. Parents can properly train, teach, and role model, but the duty of the child is to receive and implement, with a right attitude, what is presented.

God makes a point of recording this concept in the law. Paul in Ephesians 6:2 quotes Exodus 20:20—"Honor your father and mother" (this is the first commandment with a promise). The first four of the Ten Commandments deal with the vertical relationship between God and humans. Commandment number five is the one Paul is sharing with the children, and as he mentions, is the only one with a promise. The promise is not necessarily guaranteeing that the individual will live a long life, but that the corporate people of God will prosper, and stay in the land of promise, if they honor their parents. This commandment is not restricted to children for the Ten Commandments were directed to adults when given. In short, God expects children to honor their parents regardless of age.

A side note: Honoring parents that are not Christians or, worse yet, parents that are resisting their children that are trying to walk

with God, can be challenging. If you are in this difficult relationship, a friend of mine gives some excellent advice on how to honor
them. First, spend time with them. Next, serve them. Finally, pray
for them. We do not have to agree with them or accept their unbiblical critiques of our behavior or standards, but we must attempt to
honor them. These three ways seem to fulfill the requirement. Our
God is creative, and He can show us other ways to fulfill the fifth
commandment if we ask Him.

Children must be willing to humble themselves and accept their
parents' teaching and authority. God thought this process up and
gave specific responsibilities to all involved in the family structure.
The challenge to remain under authority becomes particularly difficult for children as they enter their adolescent years. However, true
Christianity should be evident and make a difference in the teenager's life as well as their parents' lives. There are no Scriptures that
clearly state that children are free to be out from under their parents' authority when they reach some arbitrary age like eighteen or
twenty-one. The break appears to happen when the child leaves the
home regardless of age.

God's Word instructs husbands to love, wives to respect, and
children to obey. If any or all of these break down, the family struggles to function. If the family is going to make an impact in the
world around us, men must seek the LORD for the grace to love and
lead as servants. Women have to search for ways to respect and to be
a source of encouragement for their men, as they make their way in
this dark world. Children have to learn how to obey their less-than-
perfect parents while still living at home and honor them for the
rest of their lives. As each one earnestly seeks to fulfill their biblical
commands, the family will thrive.

Now that we have touched on the biblical roles for each family
member, we can press on into some specifics for developing a family
philosophy. Before we do, however, I want to leave you with a few
questions to consider before the LORD in prayer and address two
more topics in the chapters that follow.

QUESTIONS TO PRAY ABOUT

Will I prayerfully consider the verses that concern me and ask the Holy Spirit to bring clarity and conviction?

As a husband, am I dying for my family as Christ did for the church?

As a wife, am I respecting my husband?

As a child, am I obeying and honoring my parents?

Will I spend time in God's Word seeking Him to know Him better?

> "The most important thing a father can do for his children is to love their mother."
>
> —Henry Ward Beecher,
> a Congregationalist clergyman from the 1800s.

Understanding Biblical Authority

And Jesus came and said to them, "All authority in heaven and on earth has been given to me.

Matthew 28:18

Authority is a word that sends the heart of every rebel into spasms, yet the Scripture has a great deal to teach on the topic by direct command and inference, and understanding this has a tremendous bearing on our quest for generational impact. Consider this seminal section from Paul's letter to the Romans.

Let every person be subject to the governing authorities. For there is no authority except from God, and those that exist have been instituted by God. Therefore whoever resists the authorities resists what God has appointed, and those who resist will incur judgment. For rulers are not a terror to good conduct, but to bad. Would you have no fear of the one who is in authority? Then do what is good, and you will receive his approval, for he is God's servant for your good. But if you do wrong, be afraid, for he does not bear the sword in vain. For he is the servant of God, an avenger who carries out God's wrath on the wrongdoer. Therefore one must be in subjection, not only to avoid God's wrath but also for the sake of conscience.

Romans 13:1–5

All authority finds its origin in God, and it is God's primary way of ruling His creation. God has established four different realms of leadership and authority—governments, families, churches, and employers. Each institution is independent and ultimately account-able to God for its actions. The head of the family answers directly to God, as does the president, boss, or pastor. Each realm of author-ity mentioned has its own jurisdiction and must not intrude into other realms. Biblically, the family has the widest level of authority, and the church, the government, and the employer must not inter-fere, unless there are sin/safety issues involved.

To illustrate, consider that God had given the right of ruler-ship to both Eli as a father and Saul as the king of Israel. In their positions, they could rule as they pleased, but they did have to be accountable to God for the way they handled their leadership posi-tions. The Scripture shows us the outcome of their rulership, and in both cases, the result was failure.

The right to rule is God given, and subjection/submission is God's plan and purpose for individuals who are under authority. I believe our understanding of this concept and subsequent actions taken toward those in authority, is an excellent barometer of our spiritual maturity.

This view of authority is not a preference but a conviction. Under-standing authority and walking it out is foundational to Christian-ity. This cannot be separated from our Christian thinking any more than my skeletal or digestive system can be removed from my body. This is a major function of the kingdom of God and its neglect and abuse has done great damage to the body of Christ. There simply is no room in God's kingdom for rebellion, lawlessness, and anarchy.

Being under authority in every area of our lives takes great faith and demonstrates the reality of our belief system. *Submission* is a word that awakens negative reactions in people. Some instantly think *dominance or doormat*; however, the word really means "being willing to line up under." In other words, it is an act of my free will to freely choose to follow someone else. No one can really force sub-mission. We can force external behavioral change, but we cannot control the inner workings of anyone. We all understand the saying "I am sitting on the outside, but I am standing up on the inside." I can outwardly comply without ever bending my will inside. Submission means that I willingly lay down my will for another. Therefore, submission to authority takes a great deal of faith, and without faith, it is impossible to please God. Ultimately, voluntarily placing yourself under a God-given authority is an act of faith in the sovereignty of God.

The *truth* of what we believe about authority will be revealed when there is a crossing of wills. Submission is something that we can say we like or agree with, but the test will come when someone in authority crosses our will. Then, what we really believe will be evident!

With that backdrop, let's move into a brief study of the Scripture. We will begin in the Old Testament first; and while this is not a complete list of verses, we can certainly gain some insight from it. Before we begin, we must understand that in the Old Testament there is a great deal of material presented, with little commentary as to whether the behaviors presented are good or not. What we are looking for, then, are principles, not necessarily rules regarding authority. Secondly, many of the men in the Old Testament lived for generations, and the overall societal structure was patriarchal with the fathers even commanding adult children and their families. I am not promoting transgenerational authority, but I am for reestablishing a proper understanding of biblical authority.

OLD TESTAMENT SCRIPTURES

In Genesis 16 we encounter the story of Sarai and Hagar. Sarai had talked Abram into a plan to help fulfill God's promise to produce an heir, which involved marriage to Sarai's slave. After the plan was executed, Sarai became extremely jealous and began to abuse her slave. Hagar and her son fled and were close to death when an angel appeared to her and had this discussion:

> The angel of the LORD found her by a spring of water in the wilderness, the spring on the way to Shur. And he said, "Hagar, servant of Sarai, where have you come from and where are you going?" She said, "I am fleeing from my mistress Sarai." The angel of the LORD said to her, "Return to your mistress and submit to her."
>
> Genesis 16:7–9

God had plans for this child, as well as Abram and Sarai, so this slave was told to return and submit to a harsh master. We are to submit to authority, even if we do not like the way we are treated. I am not saying that we must stay in a dangerous or abusive situation, but we simply cannot run away every time there is hardship. God usually has a plan that is way beyond what we can conceive.

> For I have chosen him, that he may command his children and his household after him to keep the way of the LORD by doing righteousness and justice, so that the LORD may bring to Abraham what he has promised him.
>
> Genesis 18:19

God chose Abraham and instructed him to train (command) his household in the "way of the LORD." In addition, there is the clause "so that," which would certainly seem to indicate a conditional aspect to this promise. What if Abraham failed in his God-given task? Would God have not brought Abraham into the promised land if he failed to train his family? We do not really know, but we can at least understand how important it was to God for Abraham to invest in the generations that followed. God *expected* Abraham to exercise authority in training his family to follow in the ways of the LORD.

While on the topic of Old Testament parents exercising authority over their adult children, Genesis 21, 24, 28, and 34 all contain stories and examples of parents selecting mates for their children. Again, I am not advocating that we return to that practice, but I am simply pointing out how normal it was for the one in authority to do so. Parents exercised great authority over their children even to the point of selecting their life partner. Tremendous faith would be required to trust that the one in authority was choosing wisely! Today, it would be beneficial if the young people could learn to listen to their father's advice and prayerfully consider the wisdom of his age and experience.

In Genesis chapters 42–48, we see Jacob, the patriarch, commanding his adult children to go to Egypt for grain. The men end up finding Joseph, their brother (though they do not initially know him) whom they had sold into slavery many years before. They then have to beg Jacob to send their other brother (Benjamin) down with them before they can get more food. Jacob exercised tremendous authority over his family, and they honored his wishes, more or less.

In the time of Moses, his authority was directly given from God. His task was to rule over and lead a huge number of people who had lived for generations as slaves in Egypt. The struggles were vast, and the people were very difficult to lead. Consider this passage and think about the concept of authority delegated from God to man.

> So Moses and Aaron said to all the people of Israel, "At evening you shall know that it was the LORD who brought you out of the land of Egypt, and in the morning you shall see the glory of the LORD, because he has heard your grumbling against the LORD. For what are we, that you grumble against us?" And Moses said, "When the LORD gives you in the evening meat to eat and in the morning bread to the full, because the LORD has heard your grumbling that you grumble against him—what are we? Your grumbling is not against us but against the LORD."
>
> Exodus 16:6–8

The principle to consider is that when those under authority grumbled against those in authority, they were not simply complaining about the human but against God! We must be very careful to control our frustration at those in leadership positions, for all authority ultimately comes from God's hand.

Part of what God provided for this group of suddenly free slaves was order. A slave in Egypt would have lived a lifestyle very similar to an abused dog in our day. After four hundred years of neglect and subjugation, this mass of humanity was set free in a single day.

As this mob roamed around in the desert, it would be necessary to establish some common understanding of societal decency and morals. God provided Moses with detailed instructions concerning relational issues, religious requirements, and many more laws than we can look at in this study. For our purposes, we can look at one of the "big ten." The Ten Commandments are easily recognizable, and most folks have at least heard of them, if not read them, at some point in their lifetime. It is interesting to me that the first four deal with our vertical relationship with God and the last six with how to get along with our fellow man. The middle one specifically addresses the parental relationship.

> Honor your father and your mother, that your days may be long in the land that the LORD your God is giving you.
>
> Exodus 20:12

The land was everything to the people of Israel, and God directly tied their possession of it to how they dealt with the first authority figure (parents) in their life. In fact, the next chapter of Exodus says that if a son or daughter attacked their parents or even cursed them the punishment was death! God obviously placed a premium on honoring the parental position.

While there are hundreds of Scriptures we could look at in the Old Testament, time simply will not allow. In Numbers 16 Korah and his entire family were killed for rebelling against Moses. In Numbers 30, a daughter's vow can be disallowed by her father. Deuteronomy 2 describes how a rebellious son should be dealt with by the leadership. Later in Samuel, both Eli and Samuel were rejected by God for failing to restrain their own children. King David demonstrated the proper way to handle authority—by not taking Saul's life—and the improper way to deal with sin in his own household by not dealing with his son's sinful choices. The references could continue for pages. We have not even opened the book of Proverbs, which is full of statements regarding listening and receiving instruction from those in authority. The point should be clear—God raises up people to positions of authority, and He does not take kindly to those under that authority resisting them. God has established order, and He requires His people to line up under authority.

NEW TESTAMENT SCRIPTURES

Every possible relationship regarding authority is dealt with in the New Testament. Man to God, spouses, parents, employers, civil, and church—all involve people, and there is a God-ordained order to each of them.

First, God deals with each of us as His legitimate children.

> And have you forgotten the exhortation that addresses you as sons? "My son, do not regard lightly the discipline of the LORD, nor be weary when reproved by him. For the LORD disciplines the one he loves, and chastises every son whom he receives." It is for discipline that you have to endure. God is treating you as sons. For what son is there whom his father does not discipline? If you are left without discipline, in which all have participated, then you are illegitimate children and not sons. Besides this, we have had earthly fathers who disciplined us and we respected them. Shall we not much more be subject to the Father of spirits and live? For they disciplined us for a short time as it seemed best to them, but he disciplines us for our good, that we may share his holiness.
>
> Hebrews 12:5–10

God demonstrates His authority over us by executing discipline in our lives, as a loving father should. In fact, a mark of our adoption is the very fact that we are punished by our Authority, for if we are not, then we are not truly valued. Since God is the Creator and LORD, He is entitled to our obedience, love, and worship, and He is the first authority that we must learn how to walk under. We learn to walk in submission to earthly authorities because we understand that God has delegated some of His authority to them.

Most of us would understand that God is worthy of our honor, worship, and submission, so let us move on to the other realms of authority that every one of us encounters.

GOVERNMENT AUTHORITY

In addition to the Romans passage at the beginning of this study, there are several others that relate the same principle of submission to governmental authority. Please note that each of the writers lived under complete dictators when penning these commands.

> First of all, then, I urge that supplications, prayers, intercessions, and thanksgivings be made for all people, for kings and all who are in high positions, that we may lead a peaceful and quiet life, godly and dignified in every way. This is good, and it is pleasing in the sight of God our Savior, who desires all people to be saved and to come to the knowledge of the truth.
>
> 1 Timothy 2:1–4

Paul states that how we live under authority has a direct impact on the measure of peace and quiet we have in our lives.

> Remind them to be submissive to rulers and authorities, to be obedient, to be ready for every good work, to speak evil of no one, to avoid quarreling, to be gentle, and to show perfect courtesy toward all people.
>
> Titus 3:1–2

Paul instructs his young charge that we need to be and remain submissive to authorities and to be perfectly courteous toward all. Quite a challenge, considering the current political climate we find ourselves in!

> Be subject for the Lord's sake to every human institution, whether it be to the emperor as supreme, or to governors as sent by him to punish those who do evil and to praise those

who do good. For this is the will of God, that by doing good you should put to silence the ignorance of foolish people. Live as people who are free, not using your freedom as a cover-up for evil, but living as servants of God. Honor everyone. Love the brotherhood. Fear God. Honor the emperor.

1 Peter 2:13–17

Peter was not exactly a spiritual lightweight in his own right, and he agrees with Paul—submit to those in authority. Peter even added, "Honor the emperor," and I am sure that was quite a challenge to those living under Roman oppression. Even though he was speaking to a conquered, oppressed people, Peter did not back off of the command. The rulers were entitled to honor and respect because of their position, not based on their ability or personality.

FAMILY AUTHORITY

The first authority structure everyone encounters is the family. God has clearly established a structure within the family and has specific commands for all members, which I touched on in the previous chapter. Many of these have been rejected in our day, and we are paying a huge price for these choices. There seems to be only three family categories mentioned in the Bible: husband, wife, and children. There is no age limit mentioned in any passage regarding children, and there is no category called "young adult" or "single adult." It would appear that "children" covers both male and female until they began their own home and leave the parental authority.

Two other insights regarding fathers and their children should be considered before we move on. First, how a man leads his family directly qualifies or disqualifies him for other leadership positions.

[A man desiring to be an elder] must manage his own household well, with all dignity keeping his children submissive, for if someone does not know how to manage his own household, how will he care for God's church?

1 Timothy 3:4–5

In this passage, and also in Titus, the qualification of elders are spelled out. One of the requirements that has added detail is the one dealing with the man's parenting skills. If this man failed in leading his children, how will he possibly lead the church people, whom he exercises far less authority over? A good question to be pondered in our day.

The second issue to consider regarding fathers and parenting is the ramifications of failure. The apostle Paul is famous for his lists. Several long sentences populated with horrible sins are found in his writings. Space limits our developing these listings of sins, but notice that in both of these lists that follow, "disobedient to parents" is listed right next to some horrible crimes!

> But understand this, that in the last days there will come times of difficulty. For people will be lovers of self, lovers of money, proud, arrogant, abusive, disobedient to their parents, ungrateful, unholy, heartless, unappeasable, slanderous, without self-control, brutal, not loving good, treacherous, reckless, swollen with conceit, lovers of pleasure rather than lovers of God, having the appearance of godliness, but denying its power. Avoid such people.
> Romans 1:29–31

> They were filled with all manner of unrighteousness, evil, covetousness, malice. They are full of envy, murder, strife, deceit, maliciousness. They are gossips, slanderers, haters of God, insolent, haughty, boastful, inventors of evil, disobedient to parents, foolish, faithless, heartless, ruthless.
> 2 Timothy 3:1–5

Children become disobedient to parents because the parents allow it. It is not popular in our day to even discuss the topic, but Paul (under the inspiration of the Holy Spirit) lists disobedience to parents alongside all manner of evil. Parents must teach their children to honor and respect them to help keep the children from ending up on these lists!

CHURCH AUTHORITY

The next realm of authority deals with the church realm. God's kingdom is one of order and authority, for without these, anarchy reigns. The kingdom of God is built on a different value system than the world, so the leadership is supposed to be servant oriented, not led by greed or ego. However, even those leaders who are not perfect are entitled to submission from those that are under their authority.

> Obey your leaders and submit to them, for they are keeping watch over your souls, as those who will have to give an account. Let them do this with joy and not with groaning, for that would be of no advantage to you.
> Hebrews 13:17

> So I exhort the elders among you, as a fellow elder and a witness of the sufferings of Christ, as well as a partaker in the glory that is going to be revealed: shepherd the flock of God that is among you, exercising oversight, not under compulsion, but willingly, as God would have you; not for shameful gain, but eagerly; not domineering over those in your charge, but being examples to the flock.
> 1 Peter 5:1–3

> Let the elders who rule well be considered worthy of double honor, especially those who labor in preaching and teaching.
> 1 Timothy 5:17

I will not take the space necessary to detail all of the verses (found in Timothy and Titus), but biblically, elders were to assure that there was doctrinal purity and no willful sin in those who were under their charge. Discipline could be exercised on unruly members, including public humiliation and excommunication for those who refused to come under discipline. Accusations against elders had to be weighed carefully, and rewards awaited the faithful church leader. The main point is that there is a realm of authority within the church structure, and those that lead are entitled to have followers who are willingly lining up under their leadership.

EMPLOYER AUTHORITY

The final realm of authority deals with employers. The Scripture does not have a great deal to say directly to employers and employees, but there are some principles that are clear. We are to be good workers giving a full day's work for our pay (Colossians 3:3). We are to work, or we do not eat (2 Thessalonians 3:10). Employers are to be fair and not cheat their employees (Jeremiah 22:13). In addition, if we move the discussion to slaves and masters, we would find an abundance of verses dealing with how to walk in this relationship. The one in authority was to be nonabusive, and the one under authority was to serve with a right spirit. The point for us to remember is that our bosses are authorities in our lives and are, therefore, entitled to our willingness to line up under them.

I have not presented an exhaustive listing of Scriptures dealing with this topic but certainly enough to give us an overview of the biblical stance on the topic of authority. From this overview, several things become clear: God has set up an authority structure that includes family, government, bosses, and the church. Each of these structures has a realm, and most of us are living under multiple ones, at any given time in our lives. We who are dwelling under these structures have a responsibility to willingly line up under the authority. When we refuse, we are resisting God's plan and order.

There are times of course when we must refuse to submit to authority. If the authority is asking us to sin or to violate God's Word in some fashion, then we must not obey. However, we must be ready to suffer the consequences of this disobedience when we choose not to submit. If we are in an abusive situation, and we can escape, we should. The apostle Paul told slaves to bear up, but if they could get free, to do so (1 Corinthians 7:21).

Even in difficult situations, the commands given are often "to bear up under," rather than "flee from." It seems that God is not nearly as concerned with what we go through, as He is with *our response to* what we go through. In all He allows us to experience, His chief concern is that our attitudes become Christlike, not that we necessarily have an easy path.

God repeatedly instructed people to bear up under bad, or even abusive, authority in order to accomplish a greater goal. Some examples are: Hagar; King David with Saul; Joseph, who served a wicked Pharaoh; the prophets who served wicked kings; and Daniel, who served in a wicked government. Also Jesus said to render unto Caesar (not exactly a nice man) what was his; Jesus also said to do what the religious leaders said but to not imitate their actions. Paul said you should not revile a high priest (even a corrupt one) and also wrote all those verses dealing with submission to authority, all while in a Roman prison.

If you find yourself in a very difficult situation, remember that those under authority have the God-given right to appeal to the authority and then to go over the authority's head to God with any decision they feel is unjust. Daniel and his three friends appealed to the king for an exception to his dietary law. Esther approached the king to plead for her people's life (and this was at the direction of her uncle that raised her as his own daughter) because she knew this verse:

> The king's heart is in the hand of the LORD; He directs it like a watercourse wherever he pleases.
>
> Proverbs 21:1

We can ask God to change the authority's heart, as He desires. We can have faith that the almighty, sovereign God can change any circumstance in an instant when He desires and that if He has not changed it, then He has something else for us to learn.

The question arises, when do I outgrow the need to submit to authority? The simple answer is never.

Young men, in the same way be submissive to those who are older. All of you, clothe yourselves with humility toward one another, because, "God opposes the proud but gives grace to the humble. Humble yourselves, therefore, under God's mighty hand, that he may lift you up in due time. Cast all your anxiety on him because he cares for you."

1 Peter 5:5–7

Submit to one another out of reverence for Christ.

Ephesians 5:21

The "all of you" and "one another" in the verses means each and every one of us! There is never a time when we are not under some type of authority, and most times, we will be under several different ones. We are not a lawless people demanding our own rights, but we are servants of the Most High God bowing before His will. That will is most often revealed by, and through, His delegated authorities.

The ultimate issue is one of the heart. Am I willing to submit to someone other than myself? Am I willing to allow God to work in my life and the lives of those in authority, to accomplish His plan and purposes; or will I demand to have my way and perceived rights? Will I be willing to bear up, even under an unjust authority, for the sake of the gospel; or will I demand my rights to my will and pleasure?

By demanding my own way, most of the time, I will cause damage to multitudes of people, and God still will have to work on my selfishness and pride through another situation. A good principle to follow is that if the authorities in my life are not in agreement with my actions and desires, then I need to wait and submit to them until they are in agreement or my desires change.

Being under authority takes great faith in God—not the authority—for the authority gets that authority from God, and God can change them, remove them, or harden them at His command. Selfishness and demanding my rights are not fruits of the Spirit, but having humility and submission are very good reflections of my spiritual maturity.

In conclusion regarding this pivotal topic, one of God's primary tools to shape us, change us, and reveal our true heart motives is the authorities in our lives. God has placed them and allowed them for His purposes. With faith and humility, we can walk through any difficulty that may arise. Ultimately how we respond to the earthly authority is an excellent picture of how we are responding to our heavenly authority. Please take a few moments and prayerfully consider these questions.

QUESTIONS TO PRAY ABOUT

Am I a person under authority? How do I know?

Do I bristle whenever the subject of authority is brought up? If so, why?

Have I forgiven authorities in my life that may have abused their authority?

Am I growing in this arena, or am I stagnant?

> "We must, therefore impress it upon the young that they should regard their parents as in God's stead, and remember that however lowly, poor, frail, and strange they may be, nevertheless they are father and mother given them by God. They are not to be deprived of their honor because of their conduct or their failings."
>
> —Martin Luther, *Table Talk*

GENERATIONAL WARFARE

> And the great dragon was thrown down, that ancient serpent, who is called the devil and Satan, the deceiver of the whole world—he was thrown down to the earth, and his angels were thrown down with him.
>
> Revelation 12:9

Before we continue into a discussion on more of the family philosophy details, we must look at one topic that is often overlooked to our own peril. Failure to realize this has caused vast damage and much heartache to families everywhere. Read the following Scriptures carefully and see if you can guess where I am going with them.

> For we do not wrestle against flesh and blood, but against the rulers, against the authorities, against the cosmic powers over this present darkness, against the spiritual forces of evil in the heavenly places.
>
> Ephesians 6:12

> Be sober-minded; be watchful. Your adversary the devil prowls around like a roaring lion, seeking someone to devour.
>
> 1 Peter 5:8

> Put on the whole armor of God, that you may be able to stand against the schemes of the devil.
>
> Ephesians 6:11

> Submit yourselves therefore to God. Resist the devil, and he will flee from you.
>
> James 4:7

Failure to realize that we have an enemy that hates us is foolish and potentially dangerous. Often we neglect this entire arena from either ignorance or bad doctrine. Even a casual reading of the Gospels will reveal that Jesus spent a great deal of time defeating the works of a very real devil. The apostles Peter, Paul, and James give specific warnings that should be heeded. If the devil is not real—as some liberal theologians state—why is so much space in Scripture dedicated to dealing with this topic? While it is unwise to become devil or demon focused, ignoring this issue altogether is dangerous.

In marriage, the devil specifically wants to disrupt and tear down unity between a husband and wife. He knows the devastating impact that this destroyed relationship has for future generations. The devil knows far better than we that any house that is divided is much easier prey than one that is united. If Satan can destroy the parents, the children are left vulnerable.

The Scriptures are very clear as to the danger of our adversary and the remedy to overcome him. We are in a battle for our marriages, and the next generation is at stake. We often make the mistake of believing that we are fighting each other or simply another human, but Paul instructs us as to whom we are actually fighting. While it is true that there is a human element involved, ignoring the obvious truth in Paul's words is foolish. There are "spiritual forces of evil," and there are "cosmic powers over this present darkness." Being blind or ignorant to the spiritual implications of any argument or problem is simply shortsighted. In every situation, there are at least three parties involved—God, us, and our enemy. Each of those three has a will and purpose, and we should be aware of what each one is after. God is working to bring maturity and growth. We are often focusing on ourselves and attempting to get our way; and our enemy wants to kill, steal, and destroy (see John 10:10).

Peter warns that our adversary is like a roaring lion and he is hungry to devour someone. One day my family visited a zoo, and the animals were very active. Judging from the way the lion was roaring intensely, he must have desired to make his presence known. From almost all parts of the zoo, people came running to see this magnificent beast. The sheer volume of his roar sent chills down our spines, and I was never as grateful for the invention of iron bars as right then! I remember that experience when I read Peter's warning. Some say that our foe is defeated and toothless. If that is true, then I have known many who have been gummed and the damage was immense! Peter tells us to be watchful and sober minded. If there were no danger, why would we even need to care? A roaring lion is a magnificent picture of power and danger, and Peter tells us the devil is just like a lion on the prowl with his goal being to devour us.

Peter, Paul, and James also give insight into how to defend ourselves against our adversary. We are to be on guard, wear armor, submit to God, and we are to resist our foe. This is not meant to be an in-depth teaching on spiritual warfare, simply a wakeup call to make sure we do not ignore the battle and end up being lion food! Disharmony, disunity, and divorce impacts generations, and much of it comes from a lack of understanding of our real enemy and his schemes. Couples forget that there is a real devil that hates them and wants them to fail, and we ignore or forget this truth to our own harm.

Our enemy loves to destroy homes and is extremely successful. Many surveys reveal that the divorce rate of those in the church is equivalent to the nonchurched. Men and women have bought into the lie from Satan that what really matters is personal happiness. God never promised us happiness, but He promised us joy, and there is a vast difference. One depends on circumstances, and one does not. One depends on outward events, and one springs from the inside. One is very fleeting, and one lasts for a lifetime. Happiness is fickle at best, but joy comes from the LORD's hand and will sustain us in times of crises. In our day, men and women are changing their spouses faster than some of us change our cars. Children are left in the wake of divorce and are often disabled for years. Commitments mean little, and relationships are fleeting. Children grow up in one-parent homes or multiparent homes and question if they are loved. The children wonder what they may have done to cause the breakup and often struggle with unnecessary guilt. Those who have tasted the pain and heartache of divorce could speak to this reality

much better than I can. Patterns of divorce are set early in life, and children often imitate what they experienced as young people. And our adversary just laughs.

Husbands and wives many times live in truces, not marriages. Angry words, harsh, biting comments are the norm, with rarely a thought as to the young children listening. In counseling adults, I have had many share the trauma of their childhood as they were forced to hide in their rooms while their parents yelled and screamed, wondering if their homes would make it another day. Other children are left alone for hours while the parents are out taking care of their social needs, or pursuing their pleasures, and the young ones have to wonder if they are even missed. Millions are latch key children coming home to empty homes each day. And our adversary continues to laugh.

The Bible speaks of marriage being a picture of Christ and His church in Ephesians 5:32, yet many in the body of Christ do not properly value their marriage and easily discard it. The devil hates marriage, and he is working overtime to destroy it. We must not be ignorant of his schemes! Before we begin to look at training those who come after us, we must make sure we have not allowed the enemy a place in our lives to wreak havoc.

Give no opportunity to the devil.

Ephesians 4:27

Opportunity is a word that can be translated as place or territory. The picture in my mind is that of a beachhead during wartime. The purpose of landing on an enemy's beach is to gain a foothold or to become entrenched. Once a hostile army has gained access to a beach then progress can be made inland. Now, reinforcements and supplies can easily be landed, and the enemy becomes extremely difficult to remove. As the beach is secured, more and more troops arrive, and the advancement can begin. When we allow the enemy a "place" or landing on our beach, he readily takes it, reinforces it, and quickly begins an all-out assault. Through ignorance, sin, or neglect, we can allow the enemy of our souls a "place" in our lives. Once entrenched, he will attack with the goal of destroying our marriage, the next generation, and us. We must be on guard, be alert, be sober, be diligent, and put on armor if we are to withstand this onslaught. We must repel the enemy off our beach!

While we do not need to live in fear of the devil, we are also told not to be ignorant of his schemes. The enemy wants to destroy *your* home, and as you make progress in your attempts to raise your children, the battles will intensify. We should be spending time daily in prayer for our families. Prayerlessness and lack of spiritual understanding has ruined many homes and done great damage to the next generation. We are given armor and weapons for a reason, and the reason should be clear—we are in a battle! When we forget this fact, we are already in danger of being injured and defeated.

Who would be the most damaged if your home falls apart? What would happen to your children and their children? What about your Christian testimony? The enemy wants us to focus simply on ourselves, but the truth is that many are impacted when a home falls apart. Generations are adversely affected, the name of Christ is tarnished, and we simply cannot afford to continually fall to this tactic of our adversary. We must take the battle to him. We must remove him from our spiritual beaches and begin to block his access to our lives and families.

Please take a moment, consider carefully, pray about this often-neglected topic, and see if there are any needed changes in your home. Is there any willful sin in your life that is granting the devil a "place"? Have you been unaware of the enemy's attempts to destroy you and your family?

Our adversary's primary weapons are lying and partial truths.

> He was a murderer from the beginning, and has nothing to do with the truth, because there is no truth in him. When he lies, he speaks out of his own character, for he is a liar and the father of lies.
>
> John 8:44

The way we fight lies and partial truth is with the Word of God.

> Sanctify them in the truth; your Word is truth.
>
> John 17:17

When our enemy speaks falsehoods to us, we fight him with the truth of God's Word. Have we swallowed any of the lies that are being told to us? "You would be better off with someone else" or "He is the problem" or "God wants me happy." The truth is that if you are married you are married to the right person, you would not be better off with someone else, and God wants you to have joy in your life by walking in obedience to Him. Do not settle for the lies of the destroyer, but resist him. Fill your mind with the truth of God's Word, and press on with the battle! When the enemy lies to us, we must find the truth in God's Word to fight him. If we are tempted to be unfaithful to our spouse, we should seek the truth in the Bible regarding immorality and adultery. If we consider divorce, we should find verses on God's view of divorce—for the record He hates it! (See Malachi 2:13–17.) If we become people who are saturated with truth, the lies become so much easier to spot. If we carefully and prayerfully read God's Word daily, we will be far better prepared to resist the lies of our enemy. By developing this habit, we will not be ignorant of our adversary's schemes, and we will be well practiced in turning to our Savior for help and strength when the battle rages.

Please stop a moment and prayerfully consider the following questions.

QUESTIONS TO PRAY ABOUT

Is there some willful sin or negligence in my life that the Lord wants me to deal with?

Is my marriage and family under attack? Am I aware that there is a battle for survival?

Am I entertaining any lies or partial truths from the enemy regarding my marriage or family?

Does the enemy already have a foothold on my spiritual beach?

Have I drifted from a regular time in the truth—the Word of God?

Am I resisting the enemy, or have I given up fighting?

Is my marriage a picture of Christ and the church or something less than that?

> "Wicked parents are the most notable servants of the devil in all the world and the bloodiest enemies to their children's souls. More souls are damned by God through the influences of ungodly parents—the next to them, ungodly ministers and magistrates—than by any instruments in the world besides."
>
> —Richard Baxter, Puritan preacher
> quoted from a sermon entitled "Biblical Parenthood"

UNITED WE STAND

Therefore a man shall leave his father and mother and hold fast to his wife, and the two shall become one flesh.

Ephesians 5:31

Congratulations! By obeying this verse, you had a baby! Your life will be greatly enriched if you invest the necessary time to love, discipline, and train your child. For most, the love comes very easily and is perfectly normal. Babies are cute, and there is a natural God-given attraction between baby and parent. Without the discipline and training, however, the natural feelings of love can soon turn into anger and frustration.

Instructions regarding child training usually begin with a discussion of the child, but I want to focus on parent training first. I have briefly touched on some of the important issues already—self-denial, acceptance of the importance of reaching the next generation, and the fact that God expects *us* to do the training. However, one issue often overlooked is the spirit of the home and how the marriage affects child development.

A godly marriage is the first component necessary to help in this process of child training. The ideal is of course one man and one woman for life, where both are trying to follow the LORD with all their hearts, souls, minds, and strength. Life is made up of less-than-ideal situations, and therefore it is hard to generalize about marriage in our current day. One-parent homes and multiple divorces are the norm for our modern era, and this has taken a tremendous toll on our children. For both of these difficult situations, the principles in this book can help, if followed. Loving the LORD and depending on His grace and mercy are still the keys to daily survival in life and marriage.

God designed parents—not peers, teachers, pastors, or any other adult—to be the primary role models from whom their children are to learn life's principles. I hope that you will surround your family with good role models, but the primary responsibility rests with the parents. Your child will formulate their view of God based on what they see lived in the home. No amount of preaching, reading, and lecturing will dislodge what the child actually *observes* in your home. The few minutes or hours of instruction received each week from the church will not be enough to counteract the reality demonstrated in the home by the relationship of the parents. Hypocrisy is one of the surest ways to destroy a child's faith. Most of what is truly believed in the home will be "caught" not taught. Whatever the parents *actually* value will be reinforced to the children and probably incorporated into the child's life. We all know that the old saying "Do as I say, not as I do" never really works.

All families have problems, and all marriages have times of stress, but it is how we *walk through these times* that will make a lasting impression on our children concerning the reality of the Christian faith. For the sake of the next generation, parents need to learn to love each other. My wife and I tried to teach our children how to work *through* arguments because they are a part of life. We are both strong people with strong opinions that are often stated strongly. We sometimes had "intense fellowship," and our children tasted the reality of Christ's interaction in our home. We failed often but repented quickly, and God's grace is sufficient in all matters. Children sense fakeness and will reject it, but they will be drawn to reality.

God does not demand perfection, only a willing heart to follow Him and enough humility to admit when you are in error. If the marriage is struggling, then the home will also. The devil understands that "a house divided will not stand" (Matthew 12:25). But a household that is strong has a much better chance of multiplying its effect on the world. Children who grow up in a family where the parents love each other have a great advantage over those who do not. Begin with healing the marriage, and the children will most likely heal as well. There are many resources available today to assist a struggling marriage, and if yours is hurting, please get help for the sake of the children. It is not a sign of weakness, but wisdom, to ask for help. In my years of counseling, I have found that many marriage issues can typically be traced back to unforgiveness, dashed expectations, and failure to die to self.

Hurts and wounds are common in the process of the two attempting to become one. The illustration of rapids is helpful in comprehending the struggle. Where two streams merge there is often very turbulent water and rapids. After the two bodies of water merge, the stream or river downstream usually runs deeper and calmer. The same is true with marriage. Rapids or rough water is common in marriage as the two learn how to become one. However, as the couple works through the issues, deeper, calmer relationships ensue.

We must be quick to forgive one another. We have been forgiven a great deal, and we must offer the same forgiveness to our mate. We must be willing to offer them the benefit of the doubt, just as we want them to offer it to us. When we are hurt, we must forgive. Rough water should not surprise us in the process of two becoming one. In fact, I believe God allows some of it to expose areas that we need to work on in our maturation process. Refusing to forgive, though, will lead to bitterness, which will lead to destruction. We must be quick to forgive our mates and children. God has forgiven us so much; in turn, we must forgive those around us, especially those in our home.

Dashed expectations are typically underneath many marital issues. "I expected better communication, sex, free time, and a host of other issues," explains the disillusioned husband or wife. When the above issues do not work out as I always dreamed, I become frustrated. When I am frustrated, then the natural response is to lash out at the one that disappointed me. People are humans, and all humans fail. To expect someone to be perfect or to do what only God can do is a recipe for failure. Each one of us falls short of perfection, and each of us needs God's grace to continue our walk with Him. Allowing disillusionment to remain will lead to additional frustration and heartache. We must realize that we cannot change the past or our mate. We can learn from what has transpired and hopefully have a brighter future, but we must not let our past cripple our future. If God thinks that what you are lacking and frustrated over is truly important, He will provide it in His time. We must learn to lay down our expectations at His throne and release others from their grip.

The third issue that many struggle with is the principle of death to self. Marriage is hard work, and the only way to be successful is to practice embracing the cross of Christ daily. We have to learn to esteem the other as better than ourselves and to value them higher than our own needs and desires. I have never encountered someone having severe marriage difficulties where both the husband and the wife are actually practicing self-denial. "You cannot hurt a dead man" is a true axiom. When we die to ourselves and live for Christ, we will have an entirely different viewpoint concerning our mate. When we walk in death-to-self type love, many of our marriage issues simply disappear.

Many of us have a plaque or picture bearing 1 Corinthians 13. It would be wise for us to read it often and truly think about each aspect of love that is covered in that sacred chapter. God's definition of love is not self-centered but other centered. Real love focuses on giving and not getting. Learning how to be patient, kind, not insisting on our own way, and all of the other attributes covered in that chapter takes God's grace and mercy to achieve, but they are the goal God set for His people. The pursuit of the practice of biblical love begins in the home, and it is the perfect training ground for its development. True personal fulfillment will only be experienced as we walk in love, beginning with those who are the closest to us.

> Greater love has no one than this, that someone lay down his life for his friends.
>
> John 15:13

Assuming that the marriage is functioning and that both parents are trying to follow the LORD, let us move on to some common issues faced by all parents.

One key component critical to success in the family is to make sure both parents have the same philosophy when it comes to *how* to discipline the children. Being on different pages in regard to how, when, where, and why to bring correction to your children is an invitation to fail. Children are aware of which parent is strict and which one is lenient. Children are also very adept at playing one parent against the other. What sometimes takes place is that parents will try to make up for the deficiencies they see in their mate. If one parent is overbearing, the other will often try to be very laid back. If one is a stickler for neatness and the other is not, then both will try to impart *their* view or preference on the children. Children caught in these struggles often feel confused and unsure of what is expected. Parents must talk together about what they want to accomplish and how they expect to get there before an effective plan of discipline can be implemented. An agreement must be reached as to the different philosophical approaches or confusion and tension will reign.

Children Need Consistency

Another issue that arises is a parent feeling very guilty about correcting a fault in their children when they suffer from the same one! Messiness, laziness, being rude or self-centered is hard to correct when a parent knows they struggle with the very same issue. Excusing our own faults makes it very difficult for us to correct the ones we see in our children. However, we must deal with both of them. Allowing those faults to go unchallenged in our children, or ourselves, is a mistake. Ignoring the problem will not make it go away; in fact, it often becomes even more pronounced. Part of why God gave you the child or children He did is to help *you* grow, mature, and deal with the blind spots in your own life. Children are wonderful mirrors reflecting what we cannot see in ourselves.

I also believe that many parents need to have a priority check. Consider some of the following questions and Scripture references. What is really important in light of eternity? Am I investing in the kingdom of God or the one governed by the prince of the power of the air?

> And you were dead in the trespasses and sins in which you once walked, following the course of this world, following the prince of the power of the air, the spirit that is now at work in the sons of disobedience—among whom we all once lived in the passions of our flesh, carrying out the desires of the body and the mind, and were by nature children of wrath, like the rest of mankind.
>
> Ephesians 2:1–3

What should I be doing with my time in light of trying to reach the next generation? Is giving my life for my job worth the cost? Do I really need a night out with the guys or gals? Should I be feasting on TV, sports, violence, sexually oriented materials, and other worldly activities?

> Look carefully then how you walk, not as unwise but as wise, making the best use of the time, because the days are evil. Therefore do not be foolish, but understand what the will of the LORD is.
>
> Ephesians 5:15–17

This is a principle that I believe to contain a great deal of truth—whatever we give ourselves to our children will likewise and typically in greater measure. If the pursuit of money and pleasure is our primary focus, it will very likely be our children's focus. If I am a workaholic, the odds are very good that my children will be also. If I am selfish, self-centered, lazy, gluttonous, rude, and crabby, my children probably will be also. If I am disrespectful to authorities in my life, my children will probably be disrespectful to me. God told us to "impress" His commandments on our children's hearts. Our words, actions, and priorities make an impression on our children's sensitive hearts and minds. Our children will value what we value, not what we say, but what our lives actually reveal. God has made children to be little imitators of the adults around them; we must be careful what we do, for little eyes are constantly watching.

Many years ago, I heard the statement that "children are wet cement." Wet cement is easily scarred and dries very quickly. We all have seen little handprints or footprints in cement, or someone's name in the corner of the sidewalk. These markings were made while the cement was wet and became permanent after the cement dried. We parents are often making marks of which we are unaware in our children. What we let them see, where we let them go, and how we speak to them all make marks. We need to handle our children very carefully, for the marks we make will last a lifetime. God's grace is sufficient to cover our failures, but we must not purposefully tread on this grace.

"Touching the palate" is another principle we encountered when we were beginning the journey of parenting. In ancient Israel the midwives would chew their favorite food into a paste and then touch the palate of their ward with just a bit of it. The goal was to give the child a taste for the food while they were extremely young, knowing that the child would then grow up and like the food. What are we touching our children's palate with? Are we giving them a hunger for the world or the kingdom of God? Are we directing them toward fads and worldliness or self-denial? Are we encouraging them to develop a hunger for God's Word and His work or for self-gratification and self-centeredness? We must be careful what we allow into our children's lives at a young age.

An excellent biblical principle to be observed is

> For your obedience is known to all, so that I rejoice over you, but I want you to be wise as to what is good and innocent as to what is evil.
>
> Romans 16:19

Our children will learn the sin-sick ways of the world soon enough. During their early developmental years, we should offer them a bubble of purity and innocence. By focusing on the beauty of holiness, one learns to reject the ugliness of sin. Most of us have heard how anticounterfeit forces are trained. They handle the real money over and over again so they become intimately familiar with the feel of the genuine. After they are so used to touching the real, the fake stands out clearly. What would our society be like if our children were so trained in holiness and purity that the lies of immorality and ungodliness were instantly recognized and rejected?

The decisions we make as parents when our children are young will influence them for the rest of their lives. Many parents of teenage children ask, "Where did we go wrong? My son or daughter wants nothing to do with the things of God and everything to do with the things of the world." While no two children are exactly the same, there are principles that apply to all. An evaluation of the marks we made in their "cement" and what "touched their palate" might be revealing.

I believe the first step in raising godly children is to have parents who are committed to following Christ and dying to themselves. Accept the challenge to walk in purity, sincerity, and humility before our God, and an excellent foundation for training children is established. In order to build something that will stand, the basic building blocks must be strong and secure. If the structure is built upon a base that is crooked or crumbling, what chance does the building have of remaining straight and strong?

Parents often forsake their children for jobs, ministries, sports, and pleasure, all of which pass very quickly. Men need to feel like what they do for a living is important. However, the reality is that many men soon realize that what they did for their company can, and will be, replaced shortly after they leave. I think of men I have known who worked for many years with a company and gave much of their heart and soul to it. Soon after they retired or left, it was as if they had never even been there. We can all be replaced in the work force—but never replaced in the home. Whatever we may accomplish in our jobs is nothing compared to what we can accomplish in our homes. I understand we must work to live, but we do not have to live to work. I pray we will work for what will remain after we leave this life.

The same is true for ministry within the church. Sacrificing your family for the sake of ministry is unhealthy and out of order. Our priorities should be God first, our spouse second, children third, then work, then ministry. Many would give mental assent to this order, but perhaps we need to take a good long look at our time and checkbook and be honest. Are we following this order in how we live? It is sometimes easier to invest in those that do not know us as well as our family does. We may easily receive praise and acceptance from strangers, whereas it is harder to please those that know us best. Human nature will tend to drive us toward the activities and people that make us feel better about ourselves, and avoid the difficult relationships that might be in our home. We must overcome this temptation and invest in those who are closest to us. We can and should be ministry oriented but not at the sacrifice of those God has already placed in the direct path of our lives.

All parents will fail and make many mistakes, but God has given children a tremendous capacity to forgive and forget their parents' shortcomings. The children just need to know that they are the most important priority in a parent's life next to God and their spouse. Once the parent's heart is in the right place, then we can move into child training. If you have felt any conviction from this last section, ask the LORD to cleanse you, forgive you, and give you a brand-new heart. Each day is new and full of God's mercy; do not let the mistakes of the past steal from your future with your spouse or children. Repent, receive, and be forgiven, then move on into the adventure of training.

Jeremiah, known as the weeping prophet, utters some of the greatest words in all of Scripture in Lamentations 3:22–24. May they bring comfort to all of us as we prayerfully consider them:

> The steadfast love of the LORD never ceases; His mercies never come to an end they are new every morning; great is Your faithfulness "The LORD is my portion," says my soul, "therefore I will hope in Him."

QUESTIONS TO PRAY ABOUT

How is my marriage? Is it where is should be right now? Would my spouse agree with my answer?

Am I struggling with bitterness toward my spouse or children?

Am I struggling with dashed expectations in my marriage or family?

How am I doing when it comes to death to self on a daily basis?

Have I considered what I am exposing my children to and the marks I am making on them?

What would my children say if asked if I am a practicing Christian?

Am I able to rest in God's grace each day and to receive His mercy each morning?

> "The small social units made up of family and place are now clogged or broken. The young are cut loose to drift in the sea of impersonal society. How will they learn about life, and what will they learn?"
>
> —David Wells, professor at Gordon-Conwell Theological Seminary quoted from *No Place For Truth*

God, Did You Make a Mistake?

And God blessed them. And God said to them, "Be fruitful and multiply and fill the earth..."

Genesis 1:28

If you have any children, you have probably had some thoughts like, *God, are you really sure you wanted us to multiply? Why would You want us to pass on all our faults to someone else? Now there is a new little person with not only all of my faults and quirks but also my spouse's! What have we done? We have created a mess, and it looks, sounds, and acts just like us! God have mercy.*

Sometimes we look at our offspring, and all we seem to notice is all of our (or our spouse's) defects. We see the blending of two personalities, with all the failures included, into a completely new person, and we question God's wisdom for His plan. While this view may seem harsh, many have confided in me that this is exactly how they feel.

God created man and woman, and it was His plan for them to reproduce. In the very first chapter of Genesis, God instructs the newly formed couple to be fruitful and multiply. In other words: pass on who you are. Now granted, this was before they fell into sin, but God never rescinded the principle to multiply. We are supposed to reproduce children who are in our image. We are to be godly ourselves, and we are to instill this into the next generation. This was

God's plan from creation, and nowhere did He repeal it. In fact, in the last book of the Old Testament God states,

> Did he not make them one, with a portion of the Spirit in their union? And what was the one God seeking? Godly offspring.
>   Malachi 2:15

There are many ways that God could have accomplished producing godly offspring, but the way *He chose* was to commission parents to perform this task. God's will is clear and very direct for parents—produce godly offspring. The responsibility is ours, and we must fulfill this divine directive. God knows all of our faults, personality flaws, and sins, yet His will is clear: be fruitful and multiply with all our shortcomings included! Since we cannot escape the divine decree, we had better learn how to fulfill it.

Since God knows everything and is all wise, God could have chosen many other methods to produce the human race, including continual creation by His hand, children growing under bushes, or even hanging on trees like ripe fruit. God did not choose any of those methods but chose two very flawed people to come together in an act of love and produce another human being. In God's divine plan He allows, even commands, husbands and wives to come together and produce offspring. The majesty and mystery of birth has been photographed by modern science, but the giving of life still comes from the Creator's hand.

God decided that in this way life should begin. His plans and purposes are often way beyond what we can comprehend, but what we can understand is that God values life very much and children are considered a blessing to the couples that procreate them. God knew that the best way for a child to be reared and that the quickest way for parents to grow up was through direct parental involvement.

Our loving heavenly Father did not make a mistake, but by divine decree He determined the best way for children to become godly was by the training of their parents. God not only commands us to have children but also equips us to train them.

Prayer is an important part of the Christian life and no more so than in the realm of parenting. As we observe our own weaknesses and consider the magnitude of the responsibility of child training, we must learn to cry out to God for wisdom and insight. If it is true that parenting was God's idea in the first place, then it certainly follows that logically He has a plan and a purpose for it. As we hold that first child in our arms, we begin to sense that something wonderful has happened. We marvel at the tiny fingers and toes and discuss whom the baby looks like. As time passes, it becomes obvious that this baby needs help. After hundreds of feedings and diaper changes, the baby requires more from the parents than they are able to give. In fact, children will need almost constant attention for many, many years! As our children age, our prayer life should increase in like proportion. Each day brings new challenges and reveals how desperate we are for divine guidance. Children do not come with an instruction booklet attached at birth (One of those questions I am going to ask God in the next life is, "Why not?"), yet God has a plan for each child. We as parents must discover what part we play in training this gift from God. God has delegated the responsibility to us, and we must seek Him for His plan and purposes. We should spend time with the Creator to discover what His will is for each child that He has given to us. God will give us direction if we ask Him for it, and we must ask to have any hope of being successful.

In addition to the exhortation in Malachi regarding God's desire for godly children, God has sprinkled instructions to parents throughout the Bible on how to train their children. There are many reminders to the current generation that they make sure the next generation does not forget the great and wonderful things they have seen.

> Only take care, and keep your soul diligently, lest you forget the things that your eyes have seen, and lest they depart from your heart all the days of your life. Make them known to your children and your children's children.
>
> Deuteronomy 4:9

We must make sure that we tell our children what we have seen and what we have learned in *our* walk with God. This exercise serves two purposes. First it helps us not to forget the wonderful things that God has done in our lives by reliving them (this is especially helpful during difficult times). And second, we encourage our children (and grandchildren) to experience God's faithfulness just as we did by sharing how He helped us during our hard times. God instructs the parents to make sure *they* tell the children these things—God could have supernaturally imparted it to the children if He wished, but He instructs the parents to do so and to speak often about it to children.

> You shall teach them diligently to your children, and shall talk of them when you sit in your house, and when you walk by the way, and when you lie down, and when you rise.
> Deuteronomy 6:7

This verse was one of the primary verses responsible for launching the homeschool movement in the late 1970s and early 1980s! If we really understand what this verse is saying, it is difficult to find a time when we are not teaching or training our children. The verse uses words like *diligently* and time restraints, such as "sitting, walking, lying down, and rising up"—that pretty much covers the entire day! God delegated to the parents the responsibility to make sure their children understood what He had said and what He desired. This passage ignited a quest among parents to question the delegation of the education process to the school system, even the Christian one. An honest evaluation of *how* to fulfill this command challenged a group of dedicated parents to question the way things had always been done. Parents started asking themselves, *How can we send our children away for the bulk of a day and then watch them spend their evenings completing homework and still be obeying this passage?* As if the Holy Spirit emblazoned the word *you*, many parents took up the challenge to teach their children "when *you* sit, when *you* walk, when *you* lie down, and when *you* arise." There simply did not seem to be any way to accomplish this with the children gone most of the day. There are multiple ways to educate our children, and I will cover some of these options in a later chapter. For now, the important item to remember is that God expects—demands—that *we* teach them diligently.

> Fathers, do not provoke your children to anger, but bring them up in the discipline and instruction of the LORD.
>
> Ephesians 6:4

Fathers play a key role in this entire process of generational transference of faith. In this verse, we begin to see that God commands parents to take the *responsibility* for the training of their children, and that primarily rests on the father. Parents can delegate some of the training to others, but they cannot remove the responsibility or accountability to God for their choices. If you are reading this and there is not a father in the home, take courage for God has a special promise for you.

> Father of the fatherless and protector of widows is God in His holy habitation.
>
> Psalm 68:5

God promises to fulfill the hole left through death or divorce. The task can be overwhelming as a single parent, but God's grace is sufficient and will be poured out in abundance if you will but call upon Him. This world is full of sin-scarred people, but God's mercy will help see you through, so don't give up!

God knows how easy it is for us to forget the wonderful things that He has done for each of us. God also knows how simple it is for us to forget to *tell* our children of the wonderful things He has done on our behalf. Therefore, He *commands* us to do so. God instructs us to teach, train, instruct, impress, and bring up our children on the knowledge of what He has done. We are God's mouthpiece to the next generation of His faithfulness and mercy. We are commissioned by God to make sure *our* children know about His ways, His Word, and how He deals with mankind. *We* are given this task, and God expects us to complete it. God will give us the insight, wisdom, and grace necessary to perform the task, but we must walk it out in obedience. We are in partnership with God Almighty to train the next generation. This is not some second-rate commission, but it is *the* primary order from God to all parents.

I have been a full-time pastor for many, many years, and I believe the job of parenting is more important than any other outreach of the church. Many believing parents feel they are doing little to influence their world, and sadly, this view is often reinforced from the pulpits across America. At times pressure is put on overcommitted families simply as a pitch to get people involved in the abundance of church programs offered and to justify huge budgets for staff and buildings. While buildings, staffs, and programs are not inherently evil, church leadership should consider the huge time and financial investment being made in outreach compared to the relatively small amounts spent in training parents to reach the next generation.

With the 70–90 percent failure rate of faith impartation mentioned in the first chapter, the church should perhaps reconsider its priorities. The wholesale failure of faith impartation to our youth and the rapid increase of marriages falling apart should cause a major alarm, yet it seems that relatively few are sounding the warning bells. Based on the church marketing materials that grace my mailbox practically every day, is seems little is being done to help parents be successful at this primary task. A great deal is being done to entertain the youth, but not much in the way of training families. In a later chapter, I will explain the differences between two competing church models and how a new one is making a major impact in reducing the percentages of young people leaving their parents' faith while the currently popular model continues to fail.

Many pastors bemoan the fact that Christians do not become involved in one-on-one discipleship. In fact, it is very difficult to get someone to commit to even a six-week foundational class. Yet, as parents, we have our "disciples" for eighteen or more years! There is an opportunity in every family to disciple beyond anything that any pastor could desire. I believe that if parents would simply do a good job teaching and evangelizing their children, they will have accomplished much from heaven's point of view. If we do not capture the next generation, the fruit we produced in this generation may be lost. If we do a good job of *disciplining* our children, we will have vast doors of ministry opportunities to walk through and will have fruit that remains for generations.

We must accept this challenge and commission from God. If we want the fruit of godly children, we will have to pay the price and give the time to train them, impress God's truth upon their hearts, and instruct them in His ways. If you accept this challenge, you will not be disappointed, challenged yes, but you will be accomplishing something of real, eternal value. So much of what passes as "ministry" for children in our day is really just fluff activity with little long-term fruit or value. Are giant puppets and juvenile-oriented skits really as valuable as parents spending time with their children? Are outings to amusement and water parks, concerts, or movies really helpful for young people? I am not opposed to fun, but calling an outing to these places "ministry" certainly seems inaccurate. On the other hand, parents ministering to and investing time and energy with their family can produce fruit that lasts for generations.

Before we go on, let us take a moment and thank Him for allowing us the privilege of participation in the process of parenting. In addition, pray that we would learn everything that He has for us to learn as we raise our children to His glory.

QUESTIONS TO PRAY ABOUT

Have I given thanks to God today for His plan regarding the family?

Have I accepted the responsibility to train and invest in my children?

Have I considered that God wants me to raise my children in my image and it was not a cosmic mistake?

Have I prayed today for God's directions and wisdom for each of my children?

Do I give thanks to God daily for my rich reward called children?

Have I made sure my children understand my testimony regarding salvation?

Have I shared with my children God's answers to prayer in my life?

Am I diligently teaching my children at all times?

Do I understand how important an opportunity I have in discipling my own children?

> "Ordained by God as the basic unit of human organization, the family is not only necessary for propagating the race, but is the first school of human instruction. No other structure can replace the family. Without it, our children have no moral foundation. Without it, they become moral illiterates whose only law is self."
>
> —Chuck Colson, quoted from
> *Against the Night; Living in the New Dark Ages*

CHILDREN ARE A BLESSING (REALLY THEY ARE!)

> Behold, children are a heritage from the LORD, the fruit of the womb a reward. Like arrows in the hand of a warrior are the children of one's youth. Blessed is the man who fills his quiver with them! He shall not be put to shame when he speaks with his enemies in the gate.
>
> Psalm 127:3–5

These verses are true no matter how we may feel. The conception and birth of children, until recently, was always considered a blessing given to the godly from the hand of God. These verses state that children are a reward. Our children have been given to us because God loves us, He does not hate us nor desire to frustrate us. God has handpicked our "arrows" so we can train them and then shoot them out to hit the target God has for them. God specifically selected *your* children and placed them in *your* home to help you (and them) become all that He desires. Training children will shape and focus the parent's walk with the LORD like no other tool. In our frustration of raising these arrows, we will learn to pray and cry out to God, and our relationship with Him will grow. God intended our children to be a great blessing to us, and this can be overlooked during the hard times. In our day, children are often considered a bother and distraction, but God always considered them a blessing and reward. Children today are often rejected or postponed because they are thought of as a hindrance from achieving our financial, recreational, or personal goals. The mind-set of the world has crept into the church, especially in our philosophy of having and raising children.

The verses above indicate that children are like arrows in the hand of a warrior. While there are many purposes for arrows, one of them certainly has to be that the arrow is shot out, hopefully hitting something. The temptation of those that are family oriented is to keep the arrows in the quiver as long as possible. God does not give us children to keep them at home. They are to be trained with the goal being to send them out into the world to make a mark. A warrior will make sure his arrows are ready, and then he will let them fly. A combatant would not dream of shooting a faulty arrow or one that is bent, so he will do whatever is necessary to prepare the arrow for flight. A wise parent will do the same. Arrows will only accomplish their purpose when they are removed from the quiver and given flight.

In addition, if properly trained, our children will give us a right to confront our enemies in the "gate." The gate in Scripture usually refers to the place where the rulers or judges sat. In other words, if we do a good job raising our children, we will be able to face our adversaries in any place of judgment. We will not be ashamed, but we will be able to hold our head high as those in authority evaluate our "work." An adult child who is walking with God will give his parents great cause for rejoicing and assures that his parents' credibility with their Christian message remains intact.

Many young people have confided in me that the primary reason they rejected Christianity is that the parents did not live the same way at home as they did at church. Most children recognize hypocrisy, and they will reject it quickly. If the parents' Christianity made no real, observable difference to them, why would the child want it?

Being able to rejoice over our adult children walking with God does not happen by accident. It is easy to say, "Well, it was all God's grace" when our children turn out okay. Though this a truthful statement, I have also noticed that those who invest in doing what God has commanded often end up with better fruit than those that did not give of themselves.

Tremendous amounts of prayer, self-sacrifice, time, discipline, and diligence must be extended to reap this reward. There is a price to pay to harvest the reward of wise, godly children. Self-denial and sacrifice must take place. I have heard somewhere that children spell love t-i-m-e. Raising godly young people requires vast amounts of time. The laying down of our lives is the soil in which the crop of godly young people will grow and flourish. We must have a plan and vision for this training, or it simply will not happen. There are too many distractions for each of us today for godly children to just "happen" without parental involvement. We *will* train the children that God has given to us. Some will do it with a plan and others will train through default, but we all *will* train.

> The father of the righteous will greatly rejoice; he who fathers a wise son will be glad in him. Let your father and mother be glad; let her who bore you rejoice.
>
> Proverbs 23:24–25

According to these verses, a righteous child will make her father and mother greatly rejoice. The possibility of children being righteous if left untrained is very rare. They are more likely to respond to and be absorbed in their own selfish will. While shopping, we all have probably witnessed children demonstrating obnoxious behavior that neither are a blessing nor make their parents glad. Many times, I wish I could speak to the embarrassed parent about *why* his or her child is behaving in such an ugly fashion. Often parents blame the child, but the truth is the parents are the ones who trained the child what is acceptable or not. They scream at the checkout counter because they have been allowed to scream. They hit, kick, and bite because no one has taught them otherwise. While we may feel sorry for the parent who has such a child, the blame (and solution) rests squarely on their shoulders. The parents did not train these bad behaviors *out* of the child but allowed them to develop. No one had to teach this child to behave in such a way; they came already preprogrammed with the ability to lie, steal, cheat, and act selfishly and disagreeably.

Parents must help children control themselves until they are able to do so without the parents' intervention.

Each of us must evaluate our priorities and our value system and see if it lines up with the one God revealed in His Word. The Bible states that children are a blessing, a gift from God, and that parents are required to train them. If *our* understanding, words, actions, and time investment do not agree with the Scripture, then we need to reevaluate what we say and practice.

In order for children to be a blessing and make the parents glad, proper training *must* take place. Godliness and acceptable behavior walked out in public will not simply happen by default. Many conflicts take place first, and either the parent wins or the child wins. If the child wins, both the parent and the child lose. Patterns are often set in motion during the early years of a child's life that last a lifetime.

If you have been tracking with me so far, it becomes very clear that parenting involves more than the ability to procreate. Barring any physical inabilities or use of outside means, most couples will have children. However, that does not assure that they will become good parents. Accepting the reality and challenge of raising godly children is a frightening prospect. When the baby arrives, life will never be the same. The good news is that parenting can be a joy to experience. Remember God's promise "children are a blessing and reward!" We were warned when our babies arrived, "Just you wait. They will be holy terrors." As they aged, we were told, "Just you wait until they become toddlers. Then you will understand how horrible they can be." "Just you wait until the terrible twos." "Just you wait until they are in school or become teenagers, then you will wish you never had them." I understand how parents end up feeling this way, but the reality is the problem does not rest with the age of the child but in the parents' attitude, their lack of training the children, and involvement in their lives. We enjoyed our children at every age and continue to do so today. There are always trials and difficulties, but our attitude and parental involvement determine a great deal of how we end up "feeling about parenting."

Shortly after the baby is born, most parents realize that they have begun an incredible journey. A new life is in their hands, and they are now responsible for it. My wife and I were married at a young age, and having children helped us to quickly mature. My wife matured at a faster pace, and I am forever grateful to the LORD for her influence in my life. As I held my first daughter, the reality that we were now responsible before God for this child was very sobering. We were going to be held accountable for how we trained this "arrow," and we would someday give an account to our Master for what we did with this "talent" entrusted to us. This pressure had a good result in our life; we were forced to cry out to God for help, wisdom, and mercy. The human love was there instantly for the baby, but the insight on how to raise her would come through seeking our Father's guidance. The good news is that God has given us His Word, His Spirit, and many good resources to succeed. Here is one truth that helps: God wants us to be successful. God gives us tests so we may learn how we are doing. God is so merciful that He will continue to give us the same test over and over until we finally pass it. We are in partnership with God Almighty to raise our children, and He desires even more than we do that they be godly and that we succeed as parents.

Accepting the responsibility to train our children is the first step toward doing it. We cannot delegate this duty away to anyone else including pastors, youth workers, schoolteachers, grandparents or God, though God has certainly used these sources when parents fail to fulfill their task. God has given our children to *us*, and He expects *us* to train and prepare them for the life they will lead. All of these other people can play a part, but we as the parents are ultimately responsible.

Soon after the baby is born, one reality is certain: life will rarely be simple again. Remember how if you wanted to go to the store or out to dinner you just jumped in the car and went? Forget about it! Now, there are diaper bags, playpens, toys, highchairs, and car seats to be dealt with. Simple tasks like "How do I get the groceries and the baby into the house at the same time? If I leave the baby in the car and take the bags in, that is not safe; but if I take the baby in, then I have to leave him in the house to go back to get the groceries, and that is not right either … " Life will never be the same.

As previously stated, one sobering truth is, in order to be an effective parent, self-denial must take place daily. My schedule, my needs, my desires, my dreams, my free time and my social life all become secondary to the task of raising godly children. If rearing godly children and preparing the next generation is really that important, then my "anything" is secondary to that task. Americans demand their rights, free time, social interaction, and varied pleasure. As Christians, we have one right—the right to die to self. There is a cost, and it is not painless. Jesus said the cost to follow Him was high:

> And calling the crowd to Him with His disciples, He said to them, "If anyone would come after Me, let him deny himself and take up his cross and follow Me."
>
> Mark 8:34

This price tag is magnified many times over when we embrace parenthood. As parents, we have the right to die to ourselves so our children will be trained. My interests and needs have to be evaluated in light of what God's bigger picture is for the next generation. Raising godly children takes vast amounts of time, and there is no shortcut. The reality now is that when there is someone who is depending on me; my life must not be self-centered. The first step to training godly children is to embrace this truth: my life is not my own. I must grow to the place where I am willing to spend whatever time it takes to successfully invest in the next generation.

We will be faced, from the day the baby comes into this world, with multiple decisions and choices. What we decide determines which direction we will go. If we choose to invest in training our children, we will not regret it. If we choose to ignore this task, much heartache will follow. Our vision, dreams, and goals will determine how we invest our time. We each have only twenty-four hours a day, and we make our decisions based on this reality. Whatever we choose to do with our time impacts all that we could have done or, perhaps better said, should have done.

In college, my economics professor explained the concept of "opportunity cost" to us, and it has stayed with me for life. Essentially the concept can be summed up by the following example. Money can only be spent one time. If I purchase something that costs five dollars, the true cost is not only the five dollars I spent, but everything else I *could have bought* with the money. The same is true with time. I can only spend an hour once, so in addition to how I actually did pass the time, I made a decision to pass over all the other ways in which I *could have* spent it. Having grown children, I can testify that the time passes very quickly. We must evaluate how we spend our time when our children are still under our roof. The time will come very soon when they will be gone and the opportunity to disciple them will be lost. Once our children are out of the home, we will have plenty of time to do the things that seem so important today. What really is important is investing in the next generation. I pray we understand the opportunity and what it really costs.

The time spent on training our children will reap great rewards. I cannot guarantee that you will receive this type of blessing on much else in this life. We live in a harried and hurried society that screams for our time. Almost everything today is instant—from cooking to communications. Child training is not instant in any fashion. In fact, it often is slow and tedious. Looking for instant gratification will not work in this process of training. Long-term goals, not instant progress, are the key. While progress will be seen, the battles are often methodical and drawn out. These truths fly in the face of our culture, but then again, look at what our culture is producing.

In the next chapter, we will begin the discussion on training the children in your home. Before we venture into this material, please stop for a moment and prayerfully consider the following questions.

QUESTIONS TO PRAY ABOUT

Have I given thanks to God for my "reward" today?

Do I consider my children a heritage from the LORD?

How am I doing in preparing my arrows for release from my quiver?

Do I need to be concerned about how those in authority are evaluating my work (children)?

Do I live out at home what I present to be truth out in public?

Have I been guilty of embracing any of the "just you wait" lies as mentioned in the first part of this chapter?

Have I accepted the responsibility to raise our children and not to delegate it away to others?

How am I doing on the self-sacrifice issue regarding my spouse and children?

Have I considered "opportunity cost" regarding my children?

Do I need to reevaluate my schedule and priorities in any way?

> "The home is the fundamental unit of society; and children are born into a home, into a family. There you have the circle that is to be the chief influence in their lives. There is no question about that. It is the biblical teaching everywhere, and it is always in so-called civilizations where ideas concerning the home begin to deteriorate that society ultimately disintegrates."
>
> —David Martyn Lloyd-Jones, Welsh minister quoted from his sermon entitled "Nurture and Admonition"

ALL PARENTS TRAIN

Where there is no prophetic vision the people cast off restraint.
Proverbs 29:18

The baby arrives, and joy reigns in the home...for a season. After
the newness wears off, the reality of being a parent starts to settle
in. Newborns require almost 100 percent of our attention. Soon—
after a few days, weeks, or months—most parents begin to sense
that their children have what the ancients call a "sin nature." Baby
"flesh" is just as ugly as grown-up "flesh." By "flesh" I do not mean
skin, but I mean that part of humans that we inherited from Adam
and Eve. The angry, selfish, egotistic, arrogant, pouting, demanding,
"I want what I want when I want it" part of all of us. Let me state
it again: every child that is born will be trained. Some parents will
train by default, and others will try to train by choice, but all parents *will* train their children. Each child that lives to adulthood will
reflect that training.

While children are born with a personality, each is also formed by
what is allowed to touch their lives. A child that grows up in a world
without kindness will probably not be a kind adult unless God graciously interferes. A child who is allowed to be selfish when young
will probably become a selfish adult. Sharing is a learned behavior
and not a natural trait in most children. This is simply illustrated.
Place two small children in a room with one toy that they both want
and see what happens. Very few children will willingly share without
encouragement, but they can, and should, be taught to. There will

always be exceptions to the rules, and some ignored or untrained children will be nice to be around, but why risk it? Children trained by their parents using a plan will almost always turn out better than those who are left to themselves.

An integral part of training is planning. If a parent has no idea what they want their adult children to act like, they will not know how to help them arrive at the goal. Aim at nothing, and you will always hit it. This is a cute saying but very practical when applied to child training. Here are some goals to shoot for:

> The fear of the LORD is hatred of evil. Pride and arrogance and the way of evil and perverted speech I hate.
>
> Proverbs 8:13

> Listen to advice and accept instruction, that you may gain wisdom in the future.
>
> Proverbs 19:20

> What is desirable in a man is steadfast love.
>
> Proverbs 19:22

> But let your adorning be the hidden person of the heart with the imperishable beauty of a gentle and quiet spirit, which in God's sight is very precious.
>
> 1 Peter 3:4

What would our churches look like today if they were filled with young men and women who were humble, used pure speech, and whose behavior demonstrated teachableness and respect to parents and authorities and where the men were known for their kindness and the ladies known for their sweet, gentle spirit? What would the world think about that church? What impact would these millions of godly young people have in our generation? Right now, we will never know. Unfortunately, our churches are known for gossip, slander, selfishness, wild behavior, worldliness, and entertainment-oriented youth who desperately need revival. Where did the church go wrong? Why do we not have these verses fulfilled in our day? Why are so many young people unteachable and arrogant? Why is there little hatred for what is evil?

At least part of the answer is that parents assumed their children would become Christians simply because they were born into Christian homes. Many parents believe they have Christian children by default. *I am a Christian; therefore my child is, or will be one*, the parent thinks. Children need to meet Jesus personally, for you cannot have a second-generation salvation experience. Just because a child grows up in a Christian home does not mean that he is automatically saved. Each one will still have to have a personal encounter with the LORD themselves. God does not have grandchildren!

The same is true concerning good or righteous behavior. Your children *may be* demonstrating acceptable behavior without any training from you, but most are not. They *can be* with proper training from you, and most trained children are different from the self-trained. Notice I did not say untrained. All parents train their children. Some just have a plan, and some delegate it back to the child or others. This training begins while the children are young and continues until they leave our homes. If we do not train them, who will?

Fearing the LORD, conquering pride and arrogance, hating what is evil, possessing a listening ear, being kind, and having a gentle spirit will not happen by default or by osmosis. These traits must be desired, prayed for, and trained *into* children while they are very young. Knowing what you are after in your training endeavors will greatly assist you in your evaluating how successful you are being. How do you know if your child is listening to your instruction? How can you tell if your son is growing in his kindness? Can a gentle spirit be seen or not? Is pride running rampant in your home? Is evil being hated or embraced through your lifestyle? If we do not even know what goals we are after, we will never be able to judge how we are doing in the pursuit of them.

If you have been aiming at nothing, there is still time to change your target. Re-read the above verses and ask God to give you wisdom and insight on how to begin to implement them into your children. While no one can guarantee that you will be completely successful, at least you can know what you are shooting for.

POSITIVE AND NEGATIVE TRAINING

We train our children by what we do, say, and allow. Our words, actions, and apathy have a tremendous impact on our children. If we are coarse and rude, our children will probably be also. If we are respectful, use appropriate language, and have godly core values, our children most likely will as well. What we laugh at, our children will laugh at. Do we mock or make fun of people? So will our children. Are we insensitive to others' needs and feelings? You guessed it, so will our children imitate us. Whatever we value, our children will value, at least until they are old enough to think independently.

What we say and do, our children realize is important to us, or we would not be doing or saying it. We can speak words of life, or we can spread death by what we say. Whether life or death comes out of us, our children will imitate it. Listen closely to your children's words and see if any of it sounds familiar to you. Do you hear yourself in their conversations? Do you like what you are hearing? These little mirrors are reflecting our training. God states it this way:

> Death and life are in the power of the tongue, and those who love it will eat its fruits.
>
> Proverbs 18:21

Parents have been given a great amount of influence over their children during the most formative years of their lives. What we speak can produce good fruit or bad. We as parents can inspire or depress, encourage or bring to despair, help produce greatness or promote failure. The words of our mouths carry great weight with our children, and I pray that we will use them carefully. As we taste the fruit coming from our children's mouths, we must remember where they heard it first.

Children have great memories. A harsh word spoken in anger to your child will remain with them for years. Calling our children names releases great power. Telling our children they will never amount to anything or that they are worthless will unleash great potential to achieve those results. Harsh joking or mocking can be devastating to our children. Sarcasm and subtle put-downs can turn into a festering wound of bitterness and insecurity in a child. We must be aware of the impact of our words on our children and how much they crave and value our approval. Remember how you felt when your parents spoke to you? Your children are not any different than you were. Fortunately for parents, children also have a tremendous capacity for forgiveness. Never underestimate the power of asking for forgiveness. Children need to know that you are human; your humility gives them this insight. All parents fail in some area, but God's grace is sufficient for all failures. Children naturally love their parents and respond wonderfully when parents confess their faults and ask for forgiveness.

Another dangerous area of communication is comparing one child to another child. Each child is a unique expression of potential. One child may excel athletically and another creatively; but both are given gifts from God, and one is not better than the other is. Saying to a child, "Why can't you be like your brother or sister?" carries a huge price tag of damage. Each child has strengths and weaknesses, and a wise parent will learn to deal with both without comparing the siblings.

What we permit has a tremendous impact as well. If we allow our children to fight and speak unkindly to each other, then they will do so. If we allow our children to be disrespectful to us, then they will do so. If we allow bad attitudes to remain, they will. If we allow our children to be slothful, they will. If we allow our children's sin nature to rule them, it will. Children are not born with natural restraints (remember diapers?); parents are supposed to be that restraint until the children are old enough to restrain themselves. Children are born selfish, lazy, full of pride, and generally messy. Have you ever been in a grocery store line behind a child who has not been trained at all? Have you ever come upon a mother who is counting to three at the top of her lungs as her little darling runs away? Have you ever had in your home or been to a home where the children have not been trained to respect others' property? God expects the adults to whom He gave children to train them. Children did not come already trained from the womb. Instructions were included (in the Bible), but the assembly (the training) is required by the parents.

Negative training is much easier than positive training—it simply requires apathy and allowing a child to grow up according to its own sinful nature. We train negatively when *we do nothing* to restrain our children's sinful nature.

> The rod and reproof give wisdom, but a child left to himself brings shame to his mother.
>
> Proverbs 29:15

An untrained child will grow into a self-trained teen and then usually into an undesirable adult. Children who are allowed to train themselves will bring shame to their parents. Many employers I speak with bemoan the fact that it is practically impossible to find workers with character. Why is that? I believe it is the lack of training in the home, or better put, the abundance of negative training in the home. Parents are often too busy to take the time necessary to train in a positive way. Typically an excellent work ethic is trained *into* a child, and laziness must be trained *out* of them.

Positive training takes great effort, time, and desire. Notice I did not say perfection. God never required parents to be perfect, only diligent. Training kindness into a child or selflessness, humility, compassion, diligence, and a host of other desirable characteristics takes vast amounts of time, energy, and planning.

We as parents need to evaluate what we allow into our lives for little eyes are constantly watching. Training children to desire what is good for them is a full-time job, and it runs totally against the sinful nature. Eating proper food, getting the correct amount of rest, establishing good work habits from a young age are all examples of positive training.

One tool that has revolutionized many homes is simply establishing a bedtime for the children. This small step will bring order to many struggling homes. Young children are not adults, and they should not be on the same schedule as their parents. Sending the child to bed at seven or eight p.m. will not destroy them and most likely will help them and your home life. Parents need some time to be alone, and children need the routine. Children that are allowed to establish their own bedtime will not pick what is in their best interest or the rest of the family's. Try this simple project for a week or so if your children have been in control of their sleeping schedule. Establish bedtimes for your younger children and then stick to it. Just see if there is not a change in the whole atmosphere in your home. If there is not, your household would be rare indeed! Children crave direction and enforcement of rules. In their hearts, they do not want to be in control, and they wish the parents were.

QUESTIONS TO PRAY ABOUT

Do we have a plan to train our children, or are we just coasting along?

Have I taken the time to listen to my children's conversations and to consider what they are saying and why they are saying it?

What is coming out of my mouth—words of life or death?

Have I sinned against my children somehow and not asked for forgiveness?

Who is in charge in my home—me or my children?

> "Parents who raised spiritual champions certainly placed a high premium on the spiritual development of their children. But the fascinating distinctive is that they saw themselves as the primary spiritual developers of their young ones."
>
> —George Barna,
> *Transforming Children Into Spiritual Champions*

DR. SPOCK WAS NOT A THEOLOGIAN

Beloved, do not imitate evil but imitate good.

3 John 11

I am not a big believer in the "three easy steps" philosophy. Every situation is different, and so is every family. God made each one of us unique and has a wonderful plan for each of His beloved children. However, there are principles in the Scripture that, if followed, will produce good results for every person. No two people are the same, yet Jesus told all of us to take up our cross daily and die to ourselves. Each of us walks this truth out differently, but we all are to take up a cross, and we all are to die daily. Each child and each family is different, and therefore "one size fits all" solutions do not work. What will be common in all families, though, are God's grace, prayer, effort, sweat, diligence, failure, and the need for plenty of time for communication.

One central issue that we must follow God on, and not accept the view presented by the world system that surrounds us, is how to discipline children. The Bible is very clear that *we are to* discipline our children *and* gives specific ways to do so. While not politically or socially accepted in the current climate of public opinion, the following verses are biblically correct and therefore must be considered:

Whoever spares the rod hates his son, but he who loves him is diligent to discipline him.

Proverbs 13:24

Folly is bound up in the heart of a child, but the rod of discipline drives it far from him.

Proverbs 22:15

Do not withhold discipline from a child; if you strike him with a rod, he will not die. If you strike him with the rod, you will save his soul from Sheol.

Proverbs 23:13–14

The rod and reproof give wisdom, but a child left to himself brings shame to his mother.

Proverbs 29:15

A generation or so ago, it was decided that secular psychiatrists knew better than God and burst forth on the scene with the revelation that children should not be spanked or even corrected. This "teaching" quickly spread, and now it is almost unheard of to spank a child and even considered abuse in some circles. Manipulation, threats, time-outs, and psychology have replaced biblical instruction. To even the most uneducated observer, the removing of spanking from our society has failed completely. However, the lie persists that spanking will somehow damage the child, and spanking has been equated with increasing violence and domestic abuse (which are still increasing even though the practice of spanking has been in steady decline).

Regardless of the societal pressure, I believe the Bible is true, and I know many who have spanked their children and the children are godly, nonabused, functioning members of society. Certainly, there are those who abuse their children, but spanking is not abuse if administered properly. The Bible simply states that we must use the rod to discipline our children. For thousands of years, spanking was perfectly normal and *the* acceptable way of controlling the temper tantrums of children. We must evaluate our methods and child-training philosophies to see whether they are in line with God's Word or if we have accepted human wisdom instead. To me, it is far more abusive to allow a child to live under the control of fleshly appetites than it is to help the child learn to grow in self-control.

God said use a rod, and that *is* what works best. The rod should be used instead of the hand or a belt, for the hand allows for association of pain with the parents' touch, and the belt was meant to keep up pants, not discipline children. Another reason to use the rod is that it is a neutral object that can be associated with correction and not the physical touch or presence of the parent. A child that is disciplined with the hand many times will learn to duck whenever the parent uses hand gestures or even attempts to hug the child. Fear of being struck with the hand does not encourage love and affection between the parent and child. In addition, parents often need time to calm down and deal with the situation properly. Searching for the rod can help the tension to tone a bit before dealing with the training situation at hand.

The rod size should be appropriate to the age and size of the child on which it is being administered. While pain is a byproduct of a spanking, the goal is not the infliction of it but the changing of the child's will. Only enough force should be used to bring the child's will into submission to the parent's will.

Will is *always* the issue. Whose will is going to be accomplished? The goal and ideal is that the parent should always win the battle of wills in order to be successful. When the one under authority wins the battle, we have what is commonly called rebellion and anarchy. An overthrow of authority is not in order in a Christian home. Peace will never abide in a home full of rebellious children in charge. A three-year-old tyrant is still a tyrant.

Parents are commanded to teach their children, and children are instructed to obey their parents.

> Children, obey your parents in the Lord, for this is right.
> Ephesians 6:1

> Children, obey your parents in everything, for this pleases the Lord.
> Colossians 3:20

> He must manage his own household well, with all dignity keeping his children submissive, for if someone does not know

how to manage his own household, how will he care for God's church?

1 Timothy 3:4–5

Fathers, do not provoke your children to anger, but bring them up in the discipline and instruction of the LORD.

Ephesians 6:4

God directly addresses children in two of these verses, and His will is clear—obey your parents. We have already seen that children do not do this willingly, so the parents are commanded to make sure their children obey them. In fact, it is part of the requirement to be an elder. It is interesting to me that of all the qualifications of leadership in the church, making sure your children obey you is one that has an explanation with it. It is as if the early church understood that if the man could not train his own children, how could he possibly train others? This is a direct indictment on the church leadership of today. PKs and MKs are often the most undisciplined children in the church. Why is this tolerated? Why has the church not asked the logical question that the early church took for granted? If a man's Christianity has failed at home, what gives him the right to export that example to the church? If a man is unable to have the respect and honor of his children who live with him, how can he expect to have the same from those he is in charge of in the house of God?

The bulk of child training involves wills. Children want what they want when they want it, and parents are commanded to see that they do not get it if it is bad for them or asked for in an inappropriate manner. Parents are the control over children's selfishness until they are trained to control themselves. This inevitably involves a conflict of wills. Parents must win this battle every time. Of course, no one is perfect, and there will be times when we are tired, frustrated, distracted, etc. and we will lose a battle to two, but the goal remains the same—win every time. Here is a time-tested principle that works— be very strict when the children are very young, and you will save yourself vast amounts of time and heartache when they enter youth.

I addressed the biblical principles of authority in an earlier chapter, and it is clear that learning to live under authority is a key understanding that each child must be taught. All of our lives, each of us will be under some type of authority, and God designed it so that each of us would learn how to live under authority initially in the home. Every one of us will encounter authority in the home, school, church, our work life, and daily life via police and government. Parents must teach their children to respect them and to submit to their will before they are released into the world. It is readily apparent that as a nation we have not been training our children how to submit to authority. If it is not clear to you, simply pick up any newspaper or magazine and read it.

THE ONLY WORD MY CHILD KNOWS IS NO!

Next to *Dada*, the first word a child should learn is *no*. It may seem that the *only* word they will ever learn is *no*, but time has shown this fear to be unfounded. Children learn other words soon enough, like *mine, give me, I want, it is not my fault*, etc. From the time a child starts to demonstrate a will, we must begin to train them. While the age will vary, it is not too long after they are born that the will becomes evident. Many discerning mothers can detect the difference between a cry from their baby that represents a need and one that is simply angry for not getting what it wants. The parents who give into a baby's angry scream are setting themselves up for a long, hard battle of will conquering later. If you start early to train a baby that she does not get her wants just because she is angry, it will help you a good deal when she is a toddler, and as she moves into adolescence and young adulthood.

Many unbiblical methods are in place today to attempt to train children. The truth is that most fail. Time-outs, counting, repeated threats, screaming, blackmail, bartering, and distraction techniques all have problems at the foundational level. The major issue with these techniques is that they do not deal with the root problem of the action. Remember, the root problem is *always* an issue of wills. Who is going to be in charge—you or your child? Children will step in and take leadership and control when there is a vacuum of authority. Someone must be in charge, and if the parent refuses, the child will assume the leadership.

Some of the commonly used techniques used in our day to control children include "time-outs" (placing a child on a chair or sending him to his room) simply allow the child to stew and think through what he should do next time to not be caught or allows him time to seethe in anger. "Counting" trains a child that your word does not mean anything until you reach a certain number or irritation level. Repeated threats do the same. A child quickly learns that you really do not mean what you are saying until you reach a certain pitch or a particular volume in your voice. Blackmail or bartering is simply trading one sin for another. "Please give Daddy the brush, and I will give you some candy" or "Please give Daddy the brush, and I won't tell Mommy what a bad boy you are." Distraction techniques work for a season, but soon the child will catch on and it still does not work on the basic, underlying problem. The child needs to be taught self-control and submission to authority. None of the above tactics teach this. In fact, all of them hinder.

To have hope of success, a parent must deal with root problems and the issue of wills. My will as a parent, with the God-commanded right to train my child, must be enforced. The only honest and fair way to deal with this is to train my child to listen to me the first time I say something. With this as the goal, training does not depend on how I feel or if I am angry but on what I say. This can save a child's life as well as make the home a place of peace and security. If a child is heading to the street with oncoming traffic, the parent must be able to tell them to stop and she stops. Who is going to count to three when a car is approaching to run over your child? *Stop* should mean "Stop right now."

Children desperately need someone to be in control, and God demands that the parent be that person. We must not abandon a child to lead himself or to find someone else to train him; we must do the training. A child who is trained to listen to their parents the first time they give a command is a happy, secure child. This will not happen by accident but takes repeated training and follow-through when you give a command. Your child will quickly learn *when* you really mean what you say. I believe the only proper and fair way should be to train your child to listen to you the first time you say it, not when you have to raise your voice or repeat yourself.

Children can be trained to play nicely, not to touch items, be respectful, be quiet, be kind in what they say, to pick up their toys, to share and a host of other good traits, if the parents desire to do so. There is a price to pay in order to get behavior like this. That price is time and being consistent. Having as our number one priority the training of our children as our main occupation is hard work! Training our children is more important than our social life, our hobbies, our dinner, our personal appearance, our free time, our ministry, or our plans. This training takes immense amounts of time and effort, but the reward is well worth it. To have adult children who love the LORD and who are productive members of the kingdom of God and society should be worth any price we must pay.

In order to train our children, we have to be *with* our children. Please re-read that last sentence. My often-used statement is "the difference between a well-behaved child and one that is in trouble is one thing: parental supervision." How do we know the way our child is behaving if we are not around her? Is she playing kindly? Sharing? Speaking nicely to her brother, sister, or friend? Is she displaying anger or meanness? Is she being flirtatious? Disrespectful to an authority? Watching something on TV or the computer we would not want her to see? How can we answer these questions if we are not *with* our children? I have observed many parents who send their children off by themselves for hours, and they do not have any idea how they are behaving. Children must be watched closely and trained constantly if you desire good fruit from your labors.

Parents sometimes think, *They are with good kids, so they will be fine.* I have news for you: they will not be fine if no one is watching them. I have spent the last thirty years of my life counseling parents who wonder where they went wrong. Their child grew up in a Christian home, had the best schooling and church, and still ended up getting pregnant or on drugs. How could this happen?

> The rod and reproof give wisdom, but a child left to himself brings shame to his mother.
>
> Proverbs 29:15

Children have a sin nature that must be controlled by the parents until they are old enough to control it themselves. Has it really been that long since you were a young person? Do you not remember the temptations and troubles you experienced? Do you honestly think it has gotten better since then? The Bible gives many details of real people who made very bad decisions. Are your children exempt from making the same type of choices? Children need constant supervision. Even our world system understands this principle by paying for commercials that run on the radio and TV clearly stating that parents are the "antidrug." What does that mean? These non-Christians are challenging parents to get involved in their young person's life and find out where they are going, who they are going with, and why. Unbelievers seem to understand the value of accountability and parental supervision. Do we?

As an unsupervised young person, I was usually in some sort of trouble. Experiments with smoking, drugs, shoplifting, and girls were a daily experience. I had friends, later on a car, a part-time job, and total freedom to come and go as I wished. The results were theft, drugs and alcohol abuse, sexual immorality, and a complete loss of family relationships. Beginning at age twelve, I had way too much free time and began a journey that took a huge toll on my life. By God's grace, at age seventeen He saved me, but in those five years a great deal of innocence was lost, which was never to be replaced. I believe that much of this waste could have been avoided if the principles in this book would have been followed. Our God is redemptive, and He will even take our sin and make something good out of it, but we could certainly save our children some heartache by doing a better job of supervision.

Young people today face the same challenges we did and perhaps even more. The boundaries of decency and what most consider acceptable behavior have been pushed further. It is not unusual for Christian young people to fall into sexual sin. Most pastors that I know perform very few marriage ceremonies where both of the bride and groom are virgins, even for Christian young people. This is a shame and a reflection on the job being performed by parents. Our young people are being assaulted relentlessly from TV, the Internet, and our society to cast off all moral restraint. We as parents must help them battle this onslaught. One way we can assist is to be with them, aware of who their friends are, and limit their free time. Being the peer group of your teens is a joy and delight and also wonderful protection to them from the wiles of the enemy. But before we get there, we need to start the training process when the children are very young.

QUESTIONS TO PRAY ABOUT

Have I been duped by any of the world's child training philosophies?

Do I understand that the primary battle in child training involves an issue of wills?

Do I supervise my children enough to know what they are doing and how they are doing it?

When I discipline, do I use a rod or some other method?

Am I really willing to invest the time necessary to change how we are living as a family?

Am I a rebel toward the authorities that are in my life?

> "They [the researchers] discovered that the four primary factors necessary to prevent delinquency are: the father's firm, fair, and consistent discipline; the mother's supervision and companionship during the day; the parent's demonstrated

affection for each other and for the children; and the family's spending time together in activities where all participated."

—From a 1952 research study by Sheldon and Eleanor Glueck entitled "Unraveling Juvenile Delinquency"

GOD LOVES DISCIPLINE

For the moment all discipline seems painful rather than pleasant, but later it yields the peaceful fruit of righteousness to those who have been trained by it.

Hebrews 12:11

If you are observing your children, the inevitable will happen. Your child will display behavior that is not acceptable. By starting the training process when your child is very young, you will save yourself great amounts of work later on in your efforts to control their sinful nature. As revealed in the last chapter by the Scriptures shared, I believe spanking is a normal, biblical form of discipline. I also believe that spanking should be reserved for rebellion. In addition, there are other forms of correction and discipline for lesser infractions that we will discuss later.

Rebellion is when children communicate in some fashion, "No, I will not do what you want." Now, they may say it outright, or they may say it with an attitude, or they may simply choose to disregard what you have said; but make no mistake, that is what they are saying. When there is an issue of wills, the parents must win every time. Have I said that before? Do not let your child's will be established as the final authority in these cases, but insist that your will be carried out completely without backtalk. Remember, children must be trained to carry out your wishes, and this will go against their natural desires. Granted, there are some children who are more passive and agreeable, but all children have a will that must be brought under the authority of the parents. When the inevitable conflict arises, what should be done? I am glad you asked!

The first step in training is to make sure the child understands what is expected. Most children understand much more than their parents give them credit. Toddlers understand a great deal of what you are saying. "Go get your blanket," and the child retrieves it with little difficulty. "Don't touch" or "no" is something else the child should learn very early. I have seen prewalking children told, "Do not touch the book," and they look at their parents, then at the book in question, then back at their parents, and then touch it to see what will happen to them. If nothing happens, a small victory has been won for the child but a major defeat has been had by the parent. The parent is training her child that her word means nothing. If, on the other hand, discipline follows the act of disobedience, the child learns that there are consequences to his behavior. A child learns quickly whether his parent's word can or should be trusted.

A CONFLICT EXAMPLE

Make sure your children understand what you expect by clearly telling them. If they are old enough to talk, have them repeat it back to you. If they are not yet talking, have them look you in the eyes and make sure they understand what you are saying. Remember, unless there is brain damage, the child learns very quickly what you want and knows a lot more than you think. Once the child understands and then *chooses* to disobey your will, the battle of wills begins. In the example above, the child (we will call him Bobby) understood that he was not supposed to touch the book but decided to test the parents. After the child touches the book, the parents should sharply say, "Bobby, I told you no. You need to obey Mommy (or Daddy)," and remove the child's hand from the book. Some children will respond to the verbal correction, and that is fine. Most will not. The child will again touch the book and look at the parents to see what happens next. Repeat, "I told you no and that you much obey me." What takes place next is very important and will go a long way toward establishing the spirit of your home. Another rebuke will probably not change this persistent child's behavior. Stronger methods are usually required.

I strongly recommend acquiring a "rod" very early in the child training process. Why a rod? Because that is what the Bible clearly commands, and that should be a good enough reason for Christians. We often get into failing situations when we think we know better or more than the Scripture. Reread the verses in the chapter on "The World's Ways Do Not Work." The word *rod* is used often and is there by God's design.

Children need to know what the rod is for and how it will be used. The rod should be with you always when you are training. A child will quickly understand that the rod will be administered *whenever* disobedience arises. Rods can be a dowel rod, a switch, even a wooden spoon if it is sturdy enough, but something that will inflict enough pain without causing damage to the child's physical body. The point of using the rod is to change the child's behavior, not inflict pain. Pain is simply the tool used to persuade children that the parents' will is better than their own will.

Since the child refused to leave the book alone after the rebuke, then a spanking is in order. The issue is not the book but the will. Some parents at this point think it is easier to move the book and simply avoid the conflict. While this may be true when a child is a toddler, they are setting a disastrous training process in motion. This avoidance of the conflict will tell the child that your word does not mean anything, and if he persists, he can usually get his own way. While this may seem petty when the child is a toddler, the real fruit of this will manifest itself when the child is older. If you win each battle when the child is young, you will have far fewer struggles when the child is older. The opposite is true as well; if you lose the battles when they are two, you will lose the war when they are fourteen. A properly trained toddler will grow into a delightful teenager, and a wild, selfish, uncontrolled toddler will grow into…

Another topic that arises here is the subject of grace. Wouldn't it be more Christlike to simply give the child a break and let it slide. After all, God does not always instantly deal with all of our issues. Grace is given by God, but He is perfect, understands fully the consequences of His actions, and knows completely what He is doing. We do not. I am all for grace, and each situation must be evaluated, and giving your child a break now and again during the training process certainly is acceptable. Conversely, giving grace in almost every situation because we are tired or don't want to deal with the underlying issue will not produce the type of fruit that we desire. God does give us grace; however, He never winks at sin. The price paid for our sin was high, and it should never be taken as a license to have our own way. Disciplining our children is a God-given command, and we cannot ignore it under the guise of grace. There are times when it is better to hug and laugh, but these should be the exception, not the rule.

Discipline involving spanking should be an event not a reaction. A spanking should be given in private without anyone else watching. This is a time of training, loving, and cleansing and is a very private matter. This is not a time of screaming, fighting, struggling, or providing a spectator sport for other children. Take the child to a private place, sit him down, and explain exactly what he did wrong. Young "prespeaking" children need simply to understand that obedience is the standard and they did not obey Mommy or Daddy. If they are old enough to talk, do not ask for an excuse, for you will always get one. Do not ask, "Why did you touch the book?" or "Why did you do that?" Ask, "Do you know what you did?" or "What did you do that you were told not to do?" Explain that you love your child and God requires that you make them obey. Make sure they look you in the eye and do not allow them to struggle with you. Warn them that they will get extra swats for struggling, kicking, screaming, etc., and then follow through if they do not listen. It will usually only take a time or two, and they will calm down and actually receive the spanking without a fight. A child knows when they have done something wrong; therefore, the guilt that follows must be dealt with in an appropriate manner. Spanking provides the necessary cleansing that must take place to restore the relationship between the child and parent. This principle is demonstrated in Scripture by the following:

> But your iniquities have made a separation between you and your God, and your sins have hidden his face from you so that he does not hear.
>
> Isaiah 59:2

When we sin, our relationship with our heavenly Father is hindered. We are not kicked out of the family of God, but our intimacy is damaged until we deal with the sin. A separation happens between God and us by our willful disobedience. Jesus took our shame and guilt by His death on the cross, and therefore forgiveness is available. Our responsibility is that we must confess our sins and receive forgiveness and restoration so that we can restore the lost intimacy with our Father. The same principle applies with our children's sins against us. They must be confessed and dealt with in order to regain the normal relationship. The confession of the disobedience and the subsequent discipline remove the guilt and restore the relationship. When we fail to follow this pattern, we make room for distance in our relationship between ourselves and our children. Resentment often follows, and a further breakdown of the relationship is inevitable.

On the other hand, following through with consistent discipline actually promotes closeness and love. One of our adult children came to us and said, "When we were young and every time you spanked us, you said you did it because you loved us. I didn't believe you then, but now I know you did. Thank you for spanking us!" Most parents would love to have such a conversation; we certainly did! My child's understanding of the discipline is based on the biblical principles that were commonly understood for thousands of years. Recently, many have accepted the counterfeit belief system presented by the culture around us that spanking and discipline are actually harmful to the child. Consider this verse from the book of Hebrews:

> For the LORD disciplines the one he loves, and chastises every son whom he receives. It is for discipline that you have to endure. God is treating you as sons. For what son is there whom his father does not discipline. If you are left without discipline, in which all have participated, then you are illegitimate children and not sons.
>
> Hebrews 12:6–8

Chastise is not a common word in our day, but the definition can still be found. Most dictionaries will define the word as "To punish, as by beating. To criticize severely; rebuke." I am not advocating beating children; however, I am saying that the Bible instructs us to discipline our sons and daughters and to use whatever force is necessary to win the battle of the wills. The above verses clearly state that love and chastisement go hand in hand. In addition, if discipline was not given, it was understood that the child was not even a real son or daughter, for every father disciplines the children he loves.

Fearing that our children will not love us when they grow up if we restrain and spank them is unfounded and unbiblical. Children actually feel unloved if the parents did not even care enough to tell them, no or to stop them from inappropriate behavior. Parents who fear losing their children because of disciplining them, most often do lose them to others that will challenge them. Many unrestrained young people rebel by running off to join the Marines or even extremely controlling cult groups that will offer them discipline. The child knows that he needs boundaries and will seek them out from others if parents do not provide them.

AN EXAMPLE OF HOW TO ADMINISTER A SPANKING

After an event where the child has clearly chosen to break your understood command, remove the child to a secluded place. Breathe deeply to gain self-control and try to remember the goal of what is about to happen. You are not simply inflicting pain on the child, but you are attempting to set a pattern of obedience to authority that will last the rest of the child's life. Have the child look you in the eyes and explain to them what happened and why you are going to spank them. Depending on the age of the child, either have him lie across your lap or bend over a bed or chair. Next, using a rod, firmly strike the child on the buttocks, not the legs, back, face, or any other part of the body. The number of swats should be in direct proportion to the level of disobedience. The issue is breaking the will and gaining submission, not inflicting pain and suffering on the child. A child who can speak will most likely beg for the spanking not to take place and plead that he is really sorry for the offense. The sorrow is wonderful and necessary; however, the fulfilling of the discipline is just as important. We must teach our children that there are consequences for the decisions that they make. The point of a spanking is deterrence, and the pain must be sufficient to make the child choose the parents' will over their own the next time he is faced with this choice.

Parents who complain that spanking does not work are usually not administrating it properly or consistently. A spanking is supposed to hurt. If a child laughs or acts like the spanking does not hurt, it is not being performed properly. Many parents swat a child on a diaper, and while it may sound loud, it has little effect on the child. When a child is small, the spanking should be given on the bare bottom. As the child ages, on the undergarments is sufficient. After the event, lots of hugs and kisses should be given to assure the reestablishment of the relationship. Make sure the child understands that you love them and that this ends the event. As you can tell, spankings take time and should be an event to make an impression that lasts beyond the conflict. If spankings are given when needed and consistently administered, the frequency will decline as the child ages.

We had strong-willed children (really it seems that all children are strong-willed!), and we spanked them often. One of our children needed a spanking for refusing to play nicely with a child that we were babysitting. This child of ours refused to share and was displaying a very nasty disposition. We instructed this child as to what we expected, and she refused to listen. Therefore, a spanking followed. After a discussion of what was expected, the child was marched back into the room and given the opportunity to apologize. This child folded her arms and refused. Shocked, I marched this one back into the room and gave another spanking. The scene was repeated with the opportunity to apologize given again with the same result. This little two-foot-tall rebel crossed her arms and flatly said "no." It took several spankings to break this rebellious attitude. Finally, after what seemed like hours, this child broke and gave in. I firmly believe that if we had let this child win this battle, we would have suffered significant damage in the war of wills. This was one of the defining points in this child's character development and ours. This was the only time a repeated battle was required. There were more battles but none like this one. I wonder what would have happened had we allowed this child to win. As I walk around grocery stores and see two-foot-tall rebels screaming at their mothers, I really do not have to wonder much. Such rebels are trained to be self-absorbed by the failure of their parents to restrain them. These training experiences take time, energy, and patience, but they are well worth the reward of having peaceful, obedient children. As I observe my adult children train their own children using the same techniques, my heart is warmed. All the time and effort we invested in training our children is paying dividends in the next generation.

Children are very smart and they will test the parent's resolve—sometimes just to make sure they really mean what they have said. When you begin to train your children, do not be surprised if they test you in front of people or out in public. The child wants to know how much they are really loved, and your response in these situations will communicate greatly to your children. Are you really willing to walk out of a restaurant and go home or to the car and deal with a child throwing a temper tantrum? Will you leave a cart full of groceries at the checkout to restrain a rebel? Will you deal with the bad attitude when the grandparents are over? How about when your friends are over and you are busy talking, the child wonders,

Will you stop and deal with me? Children will test your resolve and commitment to disciplining them. If we are inconsistent or lazy, the child will know it and be insecure. If we will deal with each instance of rebellion, the child will be secure and feel protected and will stop testing you as often. Children inherently want to be controlled and told what to do. God wants the parents to do it. It is a perfect match.

One question that always arises is "How old should a child be when we begin to spank, and when should we stop spanking?" I mentioned before that a discerning parent can detect when a baby is angry and when there is a legitimate need. I am not recommending that you spank babies; however, even a baby can be trained to lie still for a diaper change by simply swatting their bottom when they attempt to roll away. Certainly by the time children are mobile, they are ready to be trained, and hopefully the process is in full action before they are toddlers.

The upper age depends on the maturity level of the child involved. Modesty issues need to be considered, and the humiliation process must be evaluated when spanking an older child. A muscled young man or adolescent young lady will probably not receive much benefit from a spanking. There is no absolute answer as to an upper age when it comes to spanking. If the parents are consistent and have captured the battle of the wills while a child is young, there may not be much need for spankings after the first few years of a child's life. On the other hand, some children need firm discipline for years and years. The simple answer is, it all depends.

Is it all worth it? If you are consistent in your love and discipline, your children might just thank you when they are older. Even if they don't, God expects us to train and discipline our children. Parents who die to themselves and invest the time necessary to train their children are setting themselves up to reap a reward of a lifetime relationship with their adult children. From personal experience, I can tell you it is well worth whatever time and energy expended to have an excellent relationship with your children and grandchildren!

QUESTIONS TO PRAY ABOUT

Have I adopted the surrounding culture's view of discipline or the biblical view?

Am I willing to pray about this topic and examine the Scriptures regarding the usage of the rod?

Have I been consistent in disciplining my child or children, or am I inconsistent?

Have I been consistent with my children when the grandparents are around or when we are out to eat or at the grocery store?

Have I been afraid to confront behavior issues in my children because I don't want to lose their love or friendship?

> "Religion, by every Christian parent, is theoretically acknowledged to be the most important thing in the world. But if in practice the father appears a thousand times more anxious for the son to be a good scholar than a real Christian, and the mother more solicitous for the daughter to be a good dancer or musician than a child of God, they may teach what they like in the way of good doctrine, but they are not to look for genuine piety as the result."
>
> —John Angell James, Puritan clergyman
> quoted from his sermon entitled
> "Principle Obstacles in Bringing Up Children for Christ"

Behavioral Issues Other Than Rebellion

> My son, do not despise the LORD's discipline or be weary of His reproof, for the LORD reproves him whom He loves, as a father the son in whom he delights.
>
> Proverbs 3:11–12

Should you spank a child for any and every offense that happens? What about accidents? How do I know when my child is being a rebel or just being childish? These questions, and many more, run through most parents' minds. As I stated earlier, spanking should be reserved for rebellion. Training, however, is a continuous action. Good behavior needs to be reinforced, and unacceptable behavior must be dealt with in all its forms. Unkind words, poochy-lip disease (sometimes referred to as pouting), selfishness, not sharing, argumentative behavior, and a host of other unacceptable actions still need to be controlled and corrected.

A child, like most untrained adults, will always want to have their "flesh" gratified. Dying to self is not an inborn trait but a learned behavior that is commanded by Jesus! One fruit of the Spirit is self-control. A "self" out of control is ugly and simply not pleasant to be around. Observant parents will watch for demonstrations of the flesh and help the child learn to take that behavior to the cross of Jesus Christ. Teaching a child to think of others above their own needs takes time and effort. Explaining that Jesus wants us to share our toys with our friends and cousins takes repeated reminders.

Children are not born with internal social skills such as how to speak kindly to handicapped people or not to laugh at people who have unsightly disfigurements; their sensitive parents must train them. Manners and respectful answers do not usually come preinstalled in a toddler; they must be trained into them.

Given the coarseness of our culture, it is good to teach your children to look at you and answer "yes" or "yes, sir" or "yes, ma'am" to a question. "Yeah" is not an answer, nor is a grunt. Ask more of your children, and you will not be disappointed. If you want teenagers people will marvel at, you must begin to train them before they walk. Responsible teens are not just some fluke of good breeding, but diligent parents produce them through much effort. As stated before, God's grace plays a significant part, but I find that many times God's grace is demonstrated on behalf of those who put forth effort. I am not referring to the free gift of salvation, but to walking out our daily life in obedience. I find the more I obey, the easier the flow of God's grace in my life. I believe the same is true regarding parenting. Involved, diligent parents help increase the flow of God's grace, and negligent, uninvolved parents hinder it. Sometimes when playing a game, someone might say "lucky" when a good catch is made. A baseball player once said, "I find the more I practice, the luckier I get." The more involved and diligent the parent is, the better chance the young person will turn out with more positive characteristics than negative ones.

Start early and constantly reinforce the behavior you want, and when they are older, you will most likely get it. Make excuses for fits, pouting, and bad attitudes, and you will get the fruit of that as well. I have seen children get away with the worst behavior under the excuse of "teething" or "not feeling well." Eventually the child will have a mouth that is full of teeth, and new excuses will be invented. Do not let your child get away with pouting and having a bad attitude. Children can, and should be, trained to look the adult in the eyes and give a complete answer in a respectful tone. Accepting anything less will cause you magnified problems when children enter adolescence.

Children will have accidents and should not be punished for them. If the accident is a result of carelessness or disobedience, then that should be dealt with, but almost everyone now and then spills something. Help the child clean it up and have a good laugh. If a window gets broken, teach the child to be more careful and let them pay as much as they can toward getting it repaired. The main point is that there are consequences to our actions and children need to be taught that life principle. Accidents happen, but many can be avoided if some precautions are exercised. Teach your children to respect others' property, and you will be able to take your children with you anywhere. The opposite is also true. If you fail to train your child not to touch others' property, you will be constantly having to "childproof" every room or house you enter.

What about delayed obedience or seemingly constant forgetful-ness? The issue still revolves around the will. If you ask your children to come inside and they reply, "In a minute," they are the ones determining *when* they will obey your command. There are always circumstances that may hinder immediate obedience, but if that is the normal response to your commands, you are probably dealing with a rebellion issue. The same can be true for *constant forgetfulness*. What the child is basically saying is that what the parents want is not as important as what the child wants, so they simply forget to do what they are asked. Everyone forgets now and then, and it seems to be getting worse the older I get; however, a constant pattern of for-getfulness can be simply choosing not to consider what the parents want as important. A wise parent must discern if the child is simply suffering from "brain fog" or if this is a pattern of disrespect or dis-obedience. In either of these cases, if it becomes clear that rebellion is determined to be at the root, then corporal discipline is necessary.

For issues that are not rebellion, like laziness; disrespectfulness; failure to accomplish assigned chores or duties; interrupting while you are on the phone; being unkind to animals, siblings, or oth-ers; and a host of other nonrebellion offenses, other forms of dis-cipline should be enforced. Spanking, I believe, should be reserved for rebellion. Each of the above can rise to that level, but if rebellion is not at the root of the unacceptable behavior, lesser punishments should be used.

As children age, many options are available for punishment of unacceptable behaviors. Loss of privileges, restrictions to media, the setting aside of a favorite toy, even financial loss, all can be used effectively to communicate the consequences of unacceptable behavior and actions. Teaching our children that there is a price to pay for failure to follow the accepted standards will help them greatly as they leave our homes. The punishment should fit the violation in direct proportion. Grounding your children for a month every time they forget to take out the trash is an overreaction and will lead to bitterness. However, not being able to play a game or chat on the computer or a restriction of some other desirable activity would be appropriate.

Look for the good; deal with the unacceptable; and train, train, train. If you invest the time when the children are small, you will reap wonderful rewards when they are older. The longer you wait to begin the training process, the harder it will be. Habits are learned very quickly, unfortunately, bad ones as well as good ones. Waiting to correct a behavior that has been accepted or ignored before will take repeated effort and harder work later on. The key is parental involvement and observation. Know what your children are saying, doing, and whom they are with at all times, and you will save yourself many sorrows. Teach your children to embrace the cross of Christ at an early age, and they will be well on their way toward becoming a productive citizen of the kingdom of God.

While it may sound as if all that ever goes on in this type of home is spanking and sermons, the opposite is true. A home where the children are trained is a happy home full of joy and peace. Laughter should be in abundance, and affection should be the norm. These do not take place in a home full of rebellion and conflict but in a home full of love and discipline. Win the battle of the wills, and you will have a joyful home. Let the children rule, and your home will resemble a lot of the dysfunctional homes in America.

QUESTIONS TO PRAY ABOUT

Am I a dictator, or at the other extreme, am I too lenient when disciplining my children?

Am I training my children to embrace the cross of Christ daily or allowing them to be self-centered?

Have I made excuses for my children because I simply did not want to deal with the underlying behavior issues?

Do we laugh and enjoy one another in our home or just tolerate each other?

Are my children learning that there are consequences to their actions?

> "Don't disdain the least of your people, keep a very watchful eye over the welfare and salvation of all your household."
>
> —Augustine quoted from Of the Miseries and Ills to Which the Human Race is Justly Exposed Through the First Sin, and from Which None Can Be Delivered Save by Christ's Grace.

FIVE KEY CONCEPTS

Whoever sends a message by the hand of a fool cuts off his own feet and drinks violence.

Proverbs 26:6

DON'T SEND A FOOL ON AN ERRAND

Many years ago, my wife and I heard this verse used to explain why parents should not send older children to give instructions or to check up on younger children. Typically, the firstborn child tends to be more mature and responsible. This may be due to genetics or perhaps more likely, because the firstborn gets more direct personal attention from the parents. When the next child is born, parents have a tendency to use the firstborn as part of the "parental committee." The older child becomes the messenger, enforcer, and gofer for the parents. While this is natural and not altogether wrong, it is not the best for the other children or the firstborn. Each child the LORD gives to you deserves your attention. Delegating this to your firstborn child will deprive the younger children of the opportunity to interact with you. In addition, this will place the firstborn in a position of authority that they should not be in. You may say, "My child is not a fool," and that is correct. However, compared to you, your three-year-old or eight-year-old or teen is a fool. All your children deserve to have your attention. Sending a five-year-old to deliver a message to a three-year-old is not the best way to accomplish what you desire. Sending your older child to break up an argument between their younger siblings will not give you the insight you need. God did not tell the firstborn to be the parent; He told you. Everyone gets tired, and on occasion it is fine to teach our children to help, but children should not carry the main load in raising their siblings.

If used in this manner, the firstborn quite possibly will grow frustrated and resentful. The younger children may lose respect for you as the parent and end up resenting the older child, thus making it harder for a lifelong friendship to be developed. All children the LORD gives to you must know they are of primary importance to you. They must know you will drop whatever you are doing and take care of them. The TV should go off, the book shut, the phone hung up, and whatever else that may compete for your time placed on hold until your children are taken care of.

Older children have a tremendous opportunity to influence their younger brothers and sisters, but being a surrogate parent is not what God intended. Older children can often see where the parent has become lax in dealing with bad attitudes and behavior in the younger children. A wise parent will listen to the older children when they bring up subjects along these lines. Statements like "I was never allowed to get away with that" or "I can't believe you allow them to speak to you that way" can give the parents some insight into areas that maybe have been allowed to slip. Appealing to the oldest child to guard his behavior because his younger siblings are watching can be a powerful tool. God placed the firstborn first for a reason, to be an example for the younger ones and to help parents learn how to parent. Most of us tend to be stricter with our first child than the others that follow. Addressing this failure with your first child and apologizing is helpful and redemptive. Children know their parents are not perfect; it greatly encourages them when the parents admit it as well.

WHAT ABOUT FRIENDS?
(THE IMPORTANCE OF THE FAMILY)

Many parents worry a great deal about friendships and the social interaction of their children. I believe God has provided most of what is needed right within the family to help develop the necessary life skills to function in society. I also believe there are several lies that have been perpetrated on the home. We have been told that there is a generation gap, and we have been told that our children need many friends and activities to be happy. Sometimes I wonder if parents are not living their lives over again through their children. If a parent was unpopular growing up, she seems to want to make sure her child does not suffer the same problem, or if a parent was a successful athlete, then the child must be as well. I do not believe there is a generation gap. I believe there is a lie from the devil that convinces us that there is a gap. For thousands of years, children spent the bulk of their time with their family. A family farm or business was handed down for generations. Children, parents, grandparents, and even great-grandparents all lived in the same general area. This is still the way it is lived out in vast parts of the world. Only in the last few generations has travel opened up new horizons and the prosperity available made it possible for grandparents to move to Florida and the family to split up. Parents are told that they cannot relate to their children; grandparents choose weather patterns instead of their family, and the toll is huge on the next generation. Accumulated wisdom is lost through the miles and lack of contact. Children are taught that the family is not very important and self-gratification is what really matters.

God's plan was for each one of us to be placed in a family setting. The ideal was for one father, one mother, various brothers and sisters, and extended family to be the major impact on a child's development. I firmly believe that friends should be limited and chosen very carefully. The Scripture states it this way:

Whoever walks with the wise becomes wise, but the companion
of fools will suffer harm.

Proverbs 13:20

Do not be deceived: "Bad company ruins good morals."

1 Corinthians 15:33

Friends will either lead children to grow in their walk with God
or drag them away. Notice that good company does not corrupt
bad character. It is almost always the other way around. Allowing
children to spend a lot of unsupervised time with friends is tempt-
ing a disaster. I believe, if at all possible, families should fellowship
together. Children should not be banished to the basement or set
in front of the TV so that the adults can talk. Parents need to know
what their children are doing and how they are interacting with
their friends. A group of six-year-olds left to themselves will get into
trouble. The same is true with teenagers. Sending your children out
with their friends to run, party, and play is not wise. This principle
holds true with Internet friends as well. Do you know what your
child's Facebook account looks like? With whom are they chatting
on MySpace or Xanga or via text messaging? Are there e-mails or
texts that your children refuse to let you look at? We should know!
Children being allowed to have their own passwords that the parents are not allowed to see is a recipe for disaster. Light brings revelation, and sin loves to hide in the dark!

One exercise I have done to demonstrate this key point is to ask
a crowd, "How many of you had good friends in high school?" In
one meeting of over 1,800 people, almost every hand went up. Since
these were adults, I then asked the follow-up question, "How many
of you are still running with the same group?" Out of this vast group,
there were perhaps two or three hands. The point is that friends
come and go, even our best ones, but family is for life. Every holi-
day, birthday, wedding, funeral, and reunion, the family remains. I
believe that God has handpicked each one of us and placed us in the
family *He* desired. We could have been born (or adopted) into any
family in this world, but He placed us in the one we are in with just

the right parents and siblings. God placed your children under your care, and if He added brothers and sisters to them, they are there to help them grow and mature. God knew exactly what He was doing when He put your family together. God has a plan for each one of His children, and the family unit plays a significant role in accomplishing this plan. If you only have one child, the principle remains the same. God has a master plan, and He does not make mistakes.

Within the family unit is almost everything needed to help develop the character necessary to accomplish God's will. Of course, others will play a part, from the extended family to pastors to other adults, but the primary tool God will use is the family unit. Have you ever wondered why children who come from the same parents are so very different? Or why no people are exactly the same? If there are multiple children in the home, I bet they have very different personalities. One is probably very sensitive and caring and one is probably not. One is more outgoing and another one is shy. One is creative and one is athletic. Why did God do this, because He has some warped sense of humor? No, God knows that it takes differences to help children grow into what He desires for them. We always told our children they would grow up and most likely marry someone similar to their brother or sister in personality. That is exactly what happened! God provided the training for marriage within the family unit. Have the goal of your children being best friends, work toward that, and you will not be disappointed when they are adults.

I believe that the devil has used the lie about a generation gap for years against the church. There is not a generation gap but a lack of parental involvement and a lack of strength on the parent's part. Parents are afraid to confront their children because they feel the child will rebel. Therefore, parents allow their children too much freedom and discretion before they are ready to have it. Christians need to realize that the devil hates the family and will do whatever is necessary to destroy it. We also need to realize that as parents we are the front line of protection for our children. What we allow in the door will make a difference in the lives that live with us.

One tool our adversary uses to propagate this lie is music. For centuries, this was not an issue. Parents and children both listened to and sang the same songs. Beginning in the early part of the last century and finding its zenith in the fifties and sixties, a brand of music entered the culture and has been one of the key tools of division ever since. Weak parents allowed their children to listen to music that they hated and we have been paying a huge price ever since.

Instinctively, parents knew much of this music was wrought with rebellion and sensuality, but they were unwilling to restrain their children. Therefore, a generation grew up on rock and roll and ushered in a rebellion for which we are still paying a huge price. (I will deal with music in more detail later.) The sexual revolution and rebellion became normal, and now our schools offer condoms, instead of biblical studies, to students. Abortion on demand became a right given from the courts, and evolution has replaced the Creator.

Christian parents seem simply satisfied if their children do not get involved in drugs or can enter marriage without being pregnant. "Normal" has been redefined as being whatever is acceptable by our culture instead of by the Bible. It is now "normal" for children to rebel against their parents. Famous Christian teachers and authors state that rebellion is a normal part of growing up. I believed this lie until I started meeting adults who did not rebel. I thought, *If one didn't have to rebel, why do any have to rebel?* If there is one exception, then the "law" that "all children rebel" does not always hold true. I realized that young people did not have to rebel. I began to see the lie that the devil had thrust on the church and set out to prove it was a lie.

While all children will struggle from time to time in their walk with God, they do not have to rebel. Children need to have their own walks, and they will question what has been taught, but they do not have to rebel! Do not settle for less than the best God has for you and your children. Your children can and should enjoy the same activities, music, entertainment, and friends that you enjoy. Do not let the devil steal away your children's heart through music or bad company. Do not be afraid to confront your children, because if you do, they will respect you when they are old enough to understand why you challenged them. God did not call you to be your children's friend but their authority. Do a good job of leading and being that authority, and you will have their friendship for life. Parents that will not confront their children for fear of losing them will often end up losing their respect and their friendship.

In summary, pick your family friends carefully, and do not believe the lies from the devil. Your children will not die if they do not have dozens of friends. They will not die if they are not popular or are not going out every night of the week. Children can actually learn to love their parents and siblings and make their best friends those which they will be spending the rest of their lives with—their families. Please do not take this section to a ridiculous conclusion. Friends and activities have a place, they are simply not first place.

GIVE YOUR CHILDREN A PURPOSE TO LIVE BIGGER THAN THEIR FLESH

Ask a typical young person today what he wants to be when he grows up and you are most likely to hear "rich." The days of desiring to be a police officer, firefighter, or teacher are mostly gone. Money, pleasure, and personal satisfaction have become the gods of our days. Self-denial, service, self-sacrifice, and thinking of others first have almost disappeared. We have an opportunity to change this course of direction for the next generation. We can train our children to live for a purpose bigger than self-gratification. This process starts when the child is very young and continues through young adulthood.

Children are born selfish. Kindness is not usually an inborn trait but something that is taught to a child by their wise parents. Begin to teach a child when they are very small to share and to think of others. Teach day in and day out that as Christians we have only one guaranteed right—the right to take up our cross and die. The Bible always tells its readers to crucify their sinful desires, never to gratify them. If we train our children from the very beginning that dying to yourself is natural and expected by God, it will become second nature to them when they mature. We must teach our children to be givers. Learn to share, give, and love. This of course is easier to do if it is already established in the lifestyle of the parents.

It is not wrong to be rich; it is wrong to have being rich as a goal or god. Many people in the Bible were wealthy, and today God often uses the wealth of Christians to accomplish great works. Money is a tool, not the end goal. Just as we teach our children to use a hammer, saw, or computer, so we must teach them to use money. Jesus said it this way:

> No one can serve two masters, for either he will hate the one and love the other, or he will be devoted to the one and despise the other. You cannot serve God and money.
>
> Matthew 6:24

We are to serve God and use money, not the other way around. If we train our children to lay down their lives, they will be useful tools in the LORD's hands. There is nothing wrong with money, pleasure, or recreation; it is the excess and worship of these things that has permeated our culture, and therein lays the destruction.

Parents must give their children a bigger reason to live than their fleshly desires. Serving others, the advancement of the kingdom of God, training the next generation, and developing their relationship with God are a few good options. There is no greater way to teach this to your children than by being a good role model yourself. Children will learn what is taught by *your* lifestyle. What is truly valued in the home will be "caught" by the children. Parents who are servants and who live for others will have a much easier time teaching this to their children.

I believe all parents should pray about taking their children on a trip somewhere so that their children can see real poverty firsthand. We have been blessed to travel as a family in Mexico and China, and it was well worth the time and money. If a child sees how a lot of the world really lives, complaining will decrease and gratefulness will increase. Our children need to see the masses of lost, suffering humanity that you just do not see in many of our neighborhoods. Give your children a view of the world from the poor person's point of view. Plan a working vacation in a poor country for the sake of your children's worldview.

There is so much more to life than simply growing up, getting an education, and then working until you retire. God has an exciting plan for each one of us, and He has works for us to accomplish. Learning to die to ourselves and giving to others opens up our hearts to that work that God has for us. Wise parents will teach this to their children from the day they are born. We are part of the family of God, and we all have a place of service within it.

Older, unmarried children have a unique opportunity to invest in the lives of others. Often twenty-something-year-old sons and daughters may wonder, *Why am I not married?* While most people will marry, not all do or should. However, while your children await marriage, if that is God's will for them, they should be encouraged to invest in others. One of our children took up this challenge and made it her goal to invest in younger children. While she awaited marriage, she would use her time in reaching out to and ministering to younger children of all ages. The impact has been great! When a godly young adult reaches out to those who are younger, it means a great deal to those young people. "Why would this older girl take time out of her life to talk to me?" some have said. "When I grow up, I want to be just like her," others said. Only God really knows the impact that just this simple action will have on the following generations. When this daughter did marry at age twenty-eight, she had over forty young girls all dressed in purple singing in her wedding. She had touched multiple girls' lives by her simple action of reaching out to them.

DON'T DESIRE THE DEATH OF YOUR SON

Discipline your son, for there is hope; do not set your heart on putting him to death.

Proverbs 19:18

Children that could not be brought under their parents' control were to be taken to the city leaders and stoned to death (Exodus 21:17). The writer of Proverbs is giving some practical wisdom to the parents in the above verse. Discipline your son soon so you will not be taking him to the leaders of the city to demand his death later on! Recently, I have had several men ask to speak to me about their teenage sons and the problems they were having with them. It is as if something just happened to them one day, and now it was getting difficult. Attitudes changed, and problems surfaced that were unknown before. Their sweet, fun-loving eight- to twelve-year-old son had changed into a walking attitude. I too have joked about not understanding this verse until my children reached the teen years. Something happens to young people from around age twelve through eighteen or so, and this can be the most trying age for parents in raising their children. However, if parents have done a good job while the children are young, this can also be one of the greatest seasons of parenting.

Young people, as they reach the age of hormones, begin to need additional time for training. I was under the false impression that toddlers needed a great deal of time and effort to train. To complete the training process, even more time is required during this period of a young adult's life. Vast amounts of discussion are required, and helping your young person come to grips with adulthood provides ample discussion fodder. Independence, sexuality, outside influences, newfound freedoms, sports, boy-girl relationships, and an enhanced understanding of almost everything require a great deal of time from the parents. Young people will find the answers that they seek; wise parents will make sure that they are the source.

Here is an area that I see many parents misunderstand. Parents often "let go" of their children way before they are ready. Children need guidance and restraint during this stage of their life, and parents should be the main ones to give it. A young person who has great freedoms will usually end up in some type of difficulty. Many godly parents have had their children become pregnant out of wedlock and ask, "How could this have happened?" Or a young person from a godly home ends up in trouble with the law or on drugs or alcohol or other forms of rebellion, and the parents are shocked. Letting go of our young people before they are ready is a recipe for disaster.

Please do not accept the view that children need freedom and time away from their parents to become normal adults. Children need intense training, and the more training their parents give them, the better adults they will most likely become. I was a youth pastor for a year or so and have worked with young people for almost three decades. One of the biggest mistakes parents make is letting go of their children before they are ready. Parents allow their children to go to camps, malls, movies, overnights, and generally run freely with their friends, and they have no idea what is really going on with, or within, their child. I have seen the fruit of this premature release of children, and it is disastrous. Parents need to know what their children are doing so they can help them make good decisions. The only way to do this is to be around when the children are in situations where good decisions are critical.

Pastors, youth workers, and other adults can make an impact in the development of your child, but the parent should be the primary source. Delegation to others is part of parenting, but many Christians never even consider the quality of the person to whom they are delegating their children. Have you ever gone to a youth camp? Do you know what "supervision" means to the one in charge? I am amazed by what parents allow and then regret later on in the process. It is better to err on the side of being too strict than too lenient. Too strict does not mean being harsh, mean, or not allowing discussion but knowing where your children are, whom they are with, and what they are doing at all times. Even when your children are with someone else, you as the parent are still responsible for their actions.

Sometimes young people struggle with bad attitudes toward their parents, and there are many possible underlying root issues to consider. Parents need to work hard to discover what is really going on in the minds of our children. Is there bitterness locked away in their hearts toward you or a sibling? Is anger eating away at them for not getting what they want or felt that they deserved? Is hurt hiding in there because of your words, broken promises, or rejection from a friend? Are they involved in some sinful behavior that you are not aware of? Are they getting a bad influence from their Internet friends or perhaps feasting on violence via computer games or TV? After a careful search of these areas, if you have not discovered the problem, then I would recommend prayerfully exploring two more areas.

If none of the above endeavors produce the fruit of a better attitude, then the answer may lie in one of two areas—friends or music. Do you know with whom your child is spending time? Do you know what they are discussing, doing, and planning? Do you know what type of music they are listening to and what it is doing to their spirit? Music has always had a strong impact on people, and today's music is no exception. If you do not like the fruit you are seeing in your young person, check their friends and their music for insight. If you sense that the music is wrong, cut it off. The same is true with the friendship. There will almost certainly be some negative reaction to this decision from your child initially and may result is a major blow up. However, if the problem is in this arena, a short-term difficult relationship problem is far better than not intervening.

Music is a volatile subject in some circles and therefore must be addressed carefully. The Scripture does not specifically address the arena of music, so we have to use discernment and personal experience to formulate our opinions. I do not believe that music is amoral. The composer writes the music with a purpose in mind, and we should not ignore their intent. Music is sensual (appeals to the senses) in nature, and each artist is attempting to provoke something from their hearers with their music. I have observed for over thirty years virtually no good fruit from a saturation of certain types of music.

First, a steady diet of love songs, regardless of the genre used, promotes an illusion about relationships. The music may promote promiscuity or even despair regarding marriage. Many country music tunes focus heavily on divorce, adultery, and all manner of indulgences that simply are not healthy. We must listen to music with our spiritual "ears" tuned and not simply enjoy the feeling generated by the song. What is the author of the tune really attempting to communicate to those who listen?

Many people that are heavily involved in listening to hard, contemporary music reduce their desire to worship and cannot do so without drums and a loud, driving beat. Young people who thrive on rock music often state, "Unless the music 'moves me,' I can't get into it." A steady diet of hard music, almost without exception, has led the young person to secular music. The secular bands are better equipped and promoted, and most of the Christian rock bands are attempting to break into the secular charts anyway. So the logic always ends up, "If the Christian bands are attempting to imitate the worldly bands, why don't I just listen to the real (good) stuff, instead of this cheap imitation?"

Personally, rock music is my "Egypt" that I was gloriously delivered from when I met the LORD. The children of Israel were delivered from the hand of Pharaoh and were repeatedly told to not go back into the bondage under his hand. As a young person, rock music was everything to me. We listened to it constantly, and it was what made us distinct from the "establishment" around us. God broke into my life and replaced hard rock music with worship, and for that I am eternally grateful. Whenever I hear this type of music, my brain is flooded with the remembrance of all manner of sin and evil performed while listening to it.

Many Christian parents feed their children this music via the oldies station. Much of this music is centered on drugs, sex, and rebellion. The Beatles, ZZ Top, The Eagles, etc., are all still popular bands that many in the Christian community listen to without any discernment as to what they are feeding their children's spirits (not to mention their minds and souls). Many of the songs are drug-laced in content and sexually charged in nature. I can't listen to any of it without pictures and memories flooding my mind. Often I can't remember what I did yesterday, but I could sing these entire songs from my teens. The music has lodged itself deep in my mind, and much of it is trash.

Today, when I see a Christian band sound and look exactly like what I was delivered from, it grieves me. Christian concerts that are laced with sensual movements by the singers and screaming young people longing to touch the singers give me strong pause as to the benefit of such events. What is being birthed in these young minds by this type of music? Are "Christian mosh pits" really helpful for hormonally charged teenagers? Again, the Scripture does not specifically address the topic; however, I strongly caution against going down that path. Where did the term "rock and roll" come from anyway? It is a sexually charged term, and most young people need little encouragement in the sexual arena. Music appeals to the sensual, so I believe we must be very careful with what we allow. My appeal is not for a complete ban on music but for parents and young people to grow in discernment.

If you or your child is struggling with the desire to worship, try a "music fast." Turn off the radio or MP3 player for a week or month, and simply purge your mind of music. Fill it with the Word of God, and see if there is a difference. Many of us are afraid of silence, but we should not be, for often that is when God speaks in His still, small voice.

One other area that may be affecting the child's attitude is not having enough of your time. Make sure you allow as much time as possible to talk over life's issues with your young person. They need direction and perspective, and you are the ones to give it to them. Do you really want your teenager getting answers from another teen or the Internet?

Friends, of course, play a part in the development process of our children. How much a part is what I am asking you to consider. Peer pressure is tremendous, and I believe that parents should be the primary peers for their children. Unhealthy dependence on friends is a key factor in the failure of many young people. The opinions of the peers are elevated to the place that parents should be in—authority. It would seem to be better to maintain multiple friendships as families rather than isolating into groups away from one another.

I am always amazed as I look at today's young people who proudly proclaim that they are free from influence and peer pressure. They boldly shout that they are "doing their own thing." Nevertheless, upon closer examination, they look like clones! Everyone is pierced in the same way, wearing the same clothes, and walking and talking the same way. Where is the individual or their freedom? Typically, the young people who are secure in their relationship with their parents stands out from the crowd. Do not desire the death of your son or daughter; invest in their lives with your time and love instead of picking up rocks!

FREEDOM, JOBS, AND MONEY

Parents do not have children, raise them, and then want to keep them locked in their bedrooms for the rest of their lives. We have children so we can send them out into the world to serve the LORD.

> Behold, children are a heritage from the LORD, the fruit of the womb a reward. Like arrows in the hand of a warrior are the children of one's youth. Blessed is the man who fills his quiver with them! He shall not be put to shame when he speaks with his enemies in the gate.
>
> Psalm 127:3–5

Children are to be trained and then "shot out" into the world. This is the goal, but often parents send their children out excessively early or before they are ready. Children need to demonstrate maturity and success in small areas before bigger responsibilities are given. Our world system has artificial guidelines established to gauge maturity. Age sixteen is when you can get your driver's license, but has the child demonstrated the necessary maturity to be put them behind the wheel of a two thousand-pound machine? Age eighteen is given as the age for adulthood, but who said that is the correct age for parents to take their hands off? Why is twenty-one the magical age for children to move out? The Bible gives no such age, but the separation from parental authority seems to begin when the young person moves out and establishes their own residence.

Freedom needs to be given as a child demonstrates the maturity to handle it properly. If a child does a good job around the house and has a mature attitude toward parental authority, then they can be released into greater arenas. If a child is a rebel at home, how do you think they will handle the speed limits when they drive? How do you think they will be as employees when their boss tells them do something they do not want to do? Freedom is a privilege, not an unalienable right. As a child demonstrates the ability to handle freedom, then more can be given. Once given, it is extremely hard to take back.

People often ask about allowances and the handling of finances for children. Children need to learn how to spend, save, and give wisely, and parents are the best teachers. I do not think it is best to just give children money. They should be given chores to earn money. Even small children can empty trashcans and help around the house. Train children early that money is a reward for working, not something that you are simply entitled to because you are alive. When children earn money, teach them to tithe, save, and be generous. Money is a tool, not the answer to life's difficulties. Help your children learn to use this tool wisely from an early age. The 80/10/10 principle is a good one to follow in money. Tithe ten percent, save ten percent, and spend the other eighty percent, if necessary. Let the child feel the weight of the responsibility of making financial decisions. If the child only has enough money for one toy or doll, then they should only buy one. They will value the items they purchase with their own money more than the ones we give them.

How old should a child be when they get a job outside of the home? The answer is it depends on how mature they are and how well they have been trained. When you believe they are ready, look for a job where your child can be around godly people as much as possible. Why shelter a child until they are sixteen and then send them into the world of drugs, sex, and rock and roll music at a fast food restaurant job? Look for men in your church who own their own business and ask if your child can assist them. Many jobs can be accomplished from home, or mature young people can start their own businesses. Children will grow up and work for the rest of their lives; they do not have to be pushed prematurely into the job market. Look for creative ways to accomplish this, and you will find them.

Many wonderful character qualities can be learned from working, such as honor, integrity, truthfulness, dependability, resourcefulness, and the satisfaction of a hard day's labor. Most employers I know would love to have good workers, and they are certainly in short supply, so train your children to work well and they will have no problem finding a job when the time comes. Just be careful about how fast you push them out of the nest.

An illustration that I have heard that describes the process well is the making of a candle. A wick is dipped in hot wax and removed. When it cools, the wick is dipped and cooled again. This process is repeated until the desired size of the candle is achieved. If the wick is placed in the hot wax and never removed, it will remain a wick. The growth of the candle's size comes in the removing and allowing time to dry. Children need to be dipped in the hot wax (world) and then removed to dry (process at home). This is done repeatedly until the candle (child) is the desired size (maturity). We expose our children to the world, and then we bring them back to the home and help them understand what they saw, experienced, and felt. We attempt to answer their questions and help them prepare for the next foray into the world. We send them back again for another time, and then bring them back home to debrief. This process is repeated until our children are strong. If we simply dip our children in the world and leave them, there they most likely will not develop properly.

QUESTIONS TO PRAY ABOUT

Have I been neglecting my younger children and placing an undue burden on the older ones?

Do I know my children's friends? Are they helping or hurting our relationship, and what we are attempting to accomplish with our family vision?

Do I have access to my children's e-mail, phone logs, and computer accounts? Should I?

Do I know the type of music my children are listening to?

Do I know the plans and dreams my children have?

Have I thought through how to introduce my children into the workforce and society?

> "One ill-chosen friend of your children's may undo all the good you are the means of doing at home. It is impossible for you to be sufficiently vigilant on this point."
>
> —John Angell James, Puritan clergyman quoted from
> *Principle Obstacles in Bringing Up Children for Christ.*

COMMON PARENTAL QUESTIONS

If any of you lacks wisdom, let him ask God, who gives generously to all without reproach, and it will be given him.

James 1:5

There are many questions that typically show up in conversations as I interact with parents, and some of them will be addressed here. The truth is that there simply are far too many issues to invent an easy list of dos and don'ts. The philosophy presented in this book can be summed up with the statement that parents need to be deeply involved in their children's lives and spend whatever time is necessary to assure that the children are being trained properly. Investing time when your children are young will pay big dividends when your children are older. If you want to have a good relationship with your adult children, invest wisely in them when they are young. What is presented on the following pages is a viewpoint, and it is not meant to be a new set of laws. Each family is unique, and therefore, we must ask God what His answer is to the following questions.

SHOULD I LET MY CHILD SPEND THE NIGHT AT A FRIEND'S HOUSE?

My short answer is probably no. However, each opportunity needs to be evaluated on a case-by-case basis. If you are *100 percent* sure the family of the friend has the exact standards as you do and they are willing to supervise your child just as you would, then the answer may be yes. However, many tragedies could have been avoided by simply saying no. Child molestations, exposure to pornographic materials, and many other damaging activities have taken place in homes that are supposedly Christian. Some surveys state that up to 50 percent of all children will be molested in their lifetime. Why take the risk? What benefits are really gained from the activity anyway? Typically, the children stay up very late, end up crabby, and are often a bad influence upon one another. There are many alternatives to sending your child to someone else's house to spend the night. Taking the children home late at night (or early morning), after the families have fellowshipped, and allowing them to sleep in their own beds is a better solution than sending them off by themselves. However, if you have friends or family members that you trust completely, then perhaps that is a different matter.

WON'T I BE CONSIDERED OFFENSIVE IF I REFUSE TO LET MY CHILDREN SPEND THE NIGHT, GO TO THE MALL, JOIN THE SPORTS TEAM, PLAY IN THE NEIGHBOR'S YARD, OR...?

Yes, you will be considered offensive, but there are greater issues at stake than simply being perceived as offensive or overprotective. One way to help limit this issue is to make sure you are upfront with people when you begin to be friends. "We do not spend the night as a policy, and it is not personal" typically will help make sure the people do not feel you are rejecting them. If you do a good job of oversight with your children, you will endure some criticism from your friends and perhaps even your extended family. You will probably be accused of being overprotective, or of thinking you are so much better than everyone else is. These comments, however, are a small price to pay for doing a good job raising your children. Remember that you, not your neighbor or well-meaning family member, will stand before God and give an account of your training. People often criticize others because they feel convicted by another's actions, and the way to deal with that guilt is to find fault with what that other person or family is doing. Consider the source in all criticism. If you have a great deal of respect for the person giving the criticism, then perhaps you should listen to it. If not, then consider the source and evaluate the truth in what is being said. It has been stated somewhere that there is an element of truth in all criticism. We should evaluate what is being said and find out what percentage of the statement is true. If after we consider the statements change is necessary, then great. If not, then we do not have to feel condemned by our choice. Sometimes we simply disagree and the issue may not be right or wrong but right and left.

We always tried to have our children play in our yard under our supervision. Neighborhood children were welcome to play with our children, but we kept a close eye on what was going on. We did not let our children play for long without checking on them. One of the best investments we ever made was buying an above-ground swimming pool. We were able to properly supervise the activities and provide guidelines for what was worn. Our girls always wore a shirt and shorts over their swimming suit whenever males were around, and we were able to have some measure of control over what our son was exposed to as he entered his manhood. We tried to have a fun environment where parents felt good about letting their children play in our yard. The neighbors knew we would be supervising, and only rarely did someone complain about our children not coming to their yard. What is the opposite of being "overprotective" anyway, being "underprotective"? I prefer to think that we were being responsible parents.

WHAT ABOUT PARTICIPATION
ON SPORTS TEAMS?

Exercise is a fun and necessary part of growing up and should be enjoyed by all. Organized sports *can* be a blessing, but often they are a major hindrance to the family. Parents end up being glorified taxi cab drivers instead of active participants in their children's life. The hard truth is that most of our children will not be professional ice skaters, basketball/soccer players, gymnasts, or volleyball stars. The price that is paid by some families is tremendous. Early morning practices every day and games almost every weekend steal valuable time from the family. Undesirable influences run rampant in the sporting world. While there are desirable character traits that can be learned from team sports, some of the time what is learned is not: exclusiveness, arrogance, unkindness, and a host of other undesirable attributes can be brought home instead.

Each family will have to make a prayerful decision about their involvement in sports. We allowed the children to participate in a variety of sports, but whatever a child did, we all tried to attend and support. If one of our children played soccer, we all went to every game and every practice to show our support. If volleyball was the preference, we all went. We ended up finding Bible Quizzing, and then we all were involved with this team sport. The point was that we were a family. We would not allow our family to be divided into segregated parts. Whatever sporting or arts-type events we participated in, we did together. One of my favorite "put downs" of the Klick family went something like this: "You Klicks are so close you probably go to the mailbox together."

WHAT ABOUT MOVIES, TV, COMPUTER GAMES, SOCIAL NETWORKING, ETC.?

Supervision is still the key to all of the above. The Bible states:

> Finally, brothers, whatever is true, whatever is honorable, whatever is just, whatever is pure, whatever is lovely, whatever is commendable, if there is any excellence, if there is anything worthy of praise, think about these things.
>
> Philippians 4:8

I call this the "Philippians four eight filter." If I can run an activity through this verse, and not receive conviction, then it is probably okay to participate in without guilt. I am afraid the church has lost much of its purity, wholesomeness, and sensitivity. Many have become so calloused that the things that used to shock us do not anymore. We have become hard in many areas, and our children have lost their innocence. I am amazed at what parents allow their small children to watch. As a practice, we always previewed any movies before our children watched them. We did not, however, live in a cave or hide our children from all outside influences. Our children watched movies growing up, but we knew where to fast forward or mute when a bad word was coming. We screened what came into their lives until they were old enough to make good decisions on their own.

While TV, movies, and the Internet serve as readily available babysitters, they are not the best ones. Parents need to use discretion regarding what is watched and what is allowed into their children's hearts, minds, and souls. It is far easier to avoid ever getting the images into your mind than it is to erase the images after they are there. Children will confront evil soon enough in our world without our inviting it into our homes via media. Allowing personal TVs and computers unsupervised in the child's room is inviting disaster. Sin loves the darkness, and one way to protect our children is to keep everything in the light.

Computer games and TV can easily become an addiction. Moderation and supervision is the key to helping our children learn to use these tools instead of being controlled by them. Sometimes a "fast" is in order to cleanse the soul. Take a break for a predetermined amount of time from the activity and devote it somewhere else, like reading or playing games together as a family. There is nothing inherently wrong with using media, but it must be under the leadership of the Holy Spirit, and it should be monitored by the parents.

WHAT ABOUT FAMILY DEVOTIONS?

Some of my fondest memories are the times of sitting around in our living room reading together. We were never a very "religious" family, even though God was the center of our lives. We laughed a lot, argued a lot, and loved a lot. In other words, we were very real. When our children were still living at home, we tried to have a daily time of reading the Scripture and prayer before I left for the office. We would pick a psalm or proverb, and read it aloud and discuss it, always trying to make some practical application for our lives. Of course, there are days when life gets in the way and you cannot get together, so this is not some legalistic formula but a pattern to implement.

Often we would read together in the evening after dinner. I would read a book aloud to the family, and then we would discuss it. We picked fun stories, fantasies, end times novels, or something that I was enjoying reading at the time. I have listed a few for your consideration, in the appendix section at the end of this book. The family seemed to enjoy just listening to me read. The point is not so much *how* you do something but that you *do something* together. You will never get another chance to be with your small children for they will grow up before you know it. Take the time to enjoy each other now. I promise you will not regret it. You do not have to be a spiritual giant to lead your family, just willing to commit the time and make the effort.

Devotions do not have to be "heavy" or even overly spiritual to be effective. The Scripture and many other books can provide a great deal of material for consideration and practical discussion. Life changes quickly enough that there will never be a lack of experiences to discuss. A wise parent will use the events of the day to discuss the realities of walking with God at a level the children can grasp. The children need to see that the parents' faith in God is real and that it impacts their daily lives. Talking about the struggles faced, victories won, and even failures endured, all add a measure of reality that our children need to see. Christianity should change us at home, help us to cope with life, and be real enough for a small child to understand. If our faith does not, or cannot help us at home, then what good is it really?

If someone in your family plays the piano or some other instrument, singing and worshiping together can help keep the center of the home pointed toward the spiritual. Even if no one plays an instrument, worship CDs are readily available, and worship music should be a part of every home. We can and should teach our children how to worship, even if we cannot sing a lick. We are told to make a joyful noise, and most of us can do that! I remember with great fondness the times my children would practice on the piano and music filled our home. As they matured in their skills, they would play hymns and choruses, and my heart soared. We are going to be spending a great deal of time in eternity worshiping around the throne of God Almighty, so we should get in the habit while we are still here. Your children will love singing together, so please don't overlook this wonderful way to keep Christ in the center of your home.

WHAT ABOUT EDUCATION CHOICES?

Do we homeschool our children or let the government schools do it for us? Perhaps we should look for a small, private school to bridge the gap between these two main choices? This is not a small question, and the way we answer it depends on what our vision is for our family. Today, the educational resources and choices are abundant and growing rapidly. The Christian school movement arose to combat the government schools' indoctrination and has been around for many years now. Most Christian schools are excellent academically and are populated with godly teachers and administrators. Home education was birthed by parents wishing to maintain significant control over, not only the academics, but the influences that were impacting their children. The Scripture is silent on the topic of methodology; however, it shouts that the parents are the ones ultimately responsible for the choice made.

Parents must research their options, know their children intimately, understand the consequences for their decision, and seek the LORD diligently regarding the education of their children. Each of the three main options has strengths and weaknesses.

Government schools (notice I do not call them public) have the advantage of significant resources including books, facilities, staff, transportation, and diverse athletic and extracurricular actives for free or relatively inexpensive cost. The classrooms are typically well equipped, and the teaching staff is trained via rigorous educational programs. On the downside, however, these schools attempt to pass on worldviews that are highly offensive to many Christians, and given the nature of group dynamics, the classroom will typically gravitate to the slightly below average student. Peer dependence is often the norm, and many children are scarred for life from experiences during their years in school. In addition, the romantic interaction between boys and girls is typical and encouraged at all levels and often leads to many broken hearts and worse.

The Christian school (or smaller private one) typically provides excellent academic training often producing significantly higher scores than the government schools on standardized testing. The staff and administration usually are dedicated professionals who love the students and consider their work to be ministry. Parents who send their children to Christian schools do not have to worry about their children being exposed to the same philosophic-oriented materials presented in the government schools. The drawbacks include expensive tuition, limited sports and extracurricular activities, and the same group dynamics of classroom instruction and peer-dominated relationships in the age-segregated government schools. The romantic notion between the sexes is also dominate in this education choice.

Parents who choose to home educate their children desire to maintain a greater control over both the academic and philosophic influences their children are exposed to. Recent studies show that the home-educated children are beating the test scores of even the private schools in the nationalized testing, at costs significantly less than either of the other options. One reason is that there simply is nowhere to hide when sitting at the table with the parent. The student either knows the answer or does not. In the organized school, the ability to duck behind someone's head to avoid eye contact is routinely used to get by in the classroom. One-on-one tutoring in the home school provides immediate feedback, and the group dynamics of sinking to the middle of the class academically are avoided. Children can go as fast as they want or spend as much time as they need in order to grasp the subject at hand. Freedom of schedule and ease of communication enhance the education process. In addition, societal issues can be controlled by the parents. Children can be exposed to (or not) whatever the parents desire, whenever they deem the children ready to see or hear it, including the natural attraction between the sexes.

Some drawbacks to home education include the time drain on the parents. Significant time is invested in teaching, lesson planning, grading and evaluation of the work, outings, and curriculum evaluation. Sometimes a lack of expertise in certain subjects like math or science can also hinder the students' learning potential. Most home schools are not equipped for extracurricular activities like sports and band; however, some support groups are attempting to address this issue by pooling their resources.

We home educated our children all the way through high school. The choice to do so was made primarily because we desired to be their main influence in all matters both academic and social. The cost of time and effort is significant, and home education should not be entered into lightly. Unless you are willing to curtail your own desires and willingly die to yourself daily, choosing some other option will probably be more appropriate for your children. Our family vision was the driving force in the education decision, and so should yours be. The choice to send your children away for large parts of the day should not be made without considering the consequences of that action. As stated previously, I believe we are free to delegate away some of the duties we are given as parents, but we will never be absolved of the responsibility of that action. If you choose to delegate the education of your children to either a government or Christian school, God will still hold you responsible for what they are taught. The ultimate key will still be the amount of time that you are willing to invest in your children when they are with you. If you send them to school, then perhaps you could volunteer to be in the classroom and be involved as a support to the school or at least make sure that your evenings are free to spend time with your children.

WHAT ABOUT HIGHER EDUCATION?

Regardless of the choice a family makes on which method to use in educating their children, questions always arise dealing with post-high school education. Should I pay for my child to go to college? Christian or government run? How about distance learning? Perhaps apprenticeship or trade school would be better? Do they really need to go to college?

The answers are not simple, and they should be bathed in prayer. Since studies show a huge percentage of Christian young people

(70–90 percent) rejecting their parents' faith in their first year of college, we dare not ignore the dangers or make these decisions hastily. Most students will be bombarded with new temptations when they step foot on the college campus. Supervision will be lax, and freedoms that the student did not have at home will abound.

In the government-run and non-Christian establishments, Darwinism and an anti-Christian bias will rule. Even in more conservative schools, the tendency is to be open-minded and tolerant of many ideas that should be rejected straight out. Academia should not be entered into lightly! Even seminaries are dangerous places where many a young zealot has lost their faith by studying the writings of wily atheists.

So what is a concerned parent to do? Pray and obey. If your son or daughter is heading to a professional occupation, then higher education cannot be avoided. However, the schools should be selected carefully, and with the explosion of the Internet, many alternative choices now exist. In fact, many advanced degrees can be earned almost entirely at home. An evaluation of the goal of the education must be deeply made. Why does my son or daughter need the education? Does it really help their career path? Could the same goal be met in some other fashion such as apprenticing or through passing certification tests?

Should you pay for your children's college education? This is another question that many disagree on. From my personal observation, it seems that people place a greater value on what they pay for themselves than on something that is simply given to them. Given the dismal work ethic that many employers bemoan perhaps it would not be overly hurtful for students to pay for their own education or at least part of it. However, this decision, like so many others, must be made in light of the overall vision that you have for your family. Going to college simply because everyone else does it is not wise. Attending because God has directed should be the only reason for spending the time, resources, and exposure to temptations our children will encounter. God does have a will and He has a plan, and we must discover it for each member of our family.

WHAT ABOUT NOT-SO-CLEAR ISSUES OR GRAY ARENAS?

Parents will encounter a host of issues that fall outside of clear biblical commands. While avoiding sexual immorality is clear, what about drinking, dancing, smoking, etc.? Most young people will encounter a variety of issues that fall outside of clear commands from the pages of Scripture, and opinions will vary depending on whom they ask.

As we mature in our walk with the LORD, I firmly believe that the Holy Spirit goes deeper into our motives. Shortly after I became a believer, I quit smoking, drinking, taking drugs, and sleeping around. As the years passed, the LORD began to touch on deeper heart issues. Questions regarding "why" I did what I did kept arising. Why did I have to be the center of attention? Why did I care if the waitress thought I was funny? Why did I need to be loved by everyone? Why did I get so angry? Why, why, why? Thousands of questions arise over our lifetimes as to why we do what we do. These are excellent questions and give good insight into our spiritual maturity.

As wise parents, we should begin to have our children ask these questions as they encounter "gray areas." Why do you want to be part of the in group? Why do you want to wear that outfit? Why do you want your nose pierced? Why do you want to smoke, dance, and drink? What is your deepest reasoning for wanting these behaviors or activities? Is it to please your LORD or to be accepted by your peers? What is your motivation?

What then should our primary motivation be for our actions? Love. Jesus and the apostles Paul, Peter, and John all say that love is the ultimate goal of our lives. If I am contemplating a behavior, I should ask "Is it based in love?" If I want to wear an outfit, am I thinking of how others will be viewing it? If my participation in an activity or behavior is going to cause my brother or sister to stumble, am I free to do it anyway? The activity may be acceptable in Scripture, and I am perfectly free to participate in it, but love compels me to restrain my freedom if it hurts someone else. "If in doubt, don't" is a good principle to follow. Love, not my personal enjoyment and freedom, must be my primary goal. We as parents must challenge our children to follow this principle, and the gray areas will be easily navigated.

QUESTIONS TO PRAY ABOUT

Have I been asking God daily for wisdom regarding my parenting?

Am I willing to be offensive to someone for the sake of my children?

Are we using sports and activities to enhance our family, or are they hindering our vision?

Am I willing to use Philippians 4:8 as a filter for our entertainment activities?

Are we attempting to have a regular time together as a family around the Word of God?

Is Christ the center of our home?

> "The parent is the spiritual guardian of his children. He cannot delegate to another the responsibility that God will someday call him to account for."
>
> —W. F. Adeney from *Deuteronomy: The Pulpit Commentary*

DATING OR COURTSHIP?

He who finds a wife finds a good thing
and obtains favor from the LORD.

Proverbs 18:22

This is not a book about how to get a spouse, but it is inevitable that the discussion will come up regarding our children. What do you do with crushes, rejection, flirtation, and hormones? If you are even barely involved as a parent, you will notice that your children will be attracted to someone of the opposite sex beginning at a young age. This is a God-given desire. The attraction issue is not the problem for most parents but rather the question of what do you do with it and when. In my opinion, allowing a child to become involved with someone of the opposite sex before they are ready to get married is a tragedy waiting to happen.

Parents need to begin the discussion about what your goals are with your children in this critical area while they are young. We had two goals—moral purity and parental involvement. We began very early to tell our children that it is perfectly normal to feel attracted to someone, or to like them, but it is not okay to go anywhere with it. If God wants you to marry that person, then the desire will remain and that person will return it in the proper time. The key here is parental involvement, knowing what your child is going through, and understanding what struggles they are having will assist you in helping your children to process it all.

We often discussed the importance of not allowing yourself to be in a place of temptation, for I believe it is easier to avoid temptation than to overcome it. We had many family friends when our children were growing up that had children of the opposite sex. Many enjoyable evenings were spent with coed activities. The main way we dealt with the boy-girl issue when our children were still at home was to usually do whatever we were doing together as a family, thus allowing parental supervision. "Good children" still want to explore sexually, and they come equipped with hormones. Leaving boys and girls alone for extended periods of time is unwise, no matter how innocent you think they are.

One key to many of these difficult issues is communication. No amount of religious activity will replace the necessity of talking with your children for hours on end. In order for there to be effective relationships, vast amounts of time must be spent in discussion. There are no shortcuts to this process. If you want good fruit, you cannot get it any other way than to invest the time required.

As our children age, it becomes necessary to determine which of the two common philosophical views will be followed regarding boy-girl relationships. Since the Scripture is not clear as to the preferred method of finding a spouse, and using historical narrative to base your understanding or preference on is potentially dangerous, care must be exercised. The Benjaminites in Judges 21 captured dancing girls at a religious festival and ran off with them. Rich men would buy slaves, and many times parents would select the mate. Wives could be gained as "plunder" from war or bartered over between fathers or older brothers. Any of the above methods could be considered "biblical"; however, I would not recommend them.

The two primary choices we face in our day are dating versus some sort of courtship, and both require a bit of explanation.

Dating typical involves a young man and woman spending time together paired up with no long-term commitment or view toward marriage. A different guy or girl could pair up each night or weekend and go to a movie or out to eat for the sheer fun of it. Perhaps it will lead to a deeper commitment or maybe not. The point is to enjoy the time together and see what happens. After dating for a time, marriage may become the goal of the relationship, but it is not the initial one.

Courtship typically involves a couple not pairing up unless marriage is the ultimate goal. There are as many understandings of courtship as there are of dating. Some parents are very involved, and others are not. Some lean to prearranged marriages, and some to a more flexible system. The main difference between courtship and dating is the end goal of the pairing of the couple.

For our family, we chose a courtship understanding, in light of our two goals stated previously—moral purity and parental involvement. We began to discuss this process with our children when they were young, and they were in total agreement with the concept of courtship. We shared with them the failures we had experienced when we were dating and why we wanted to help them go a different direction. It is best to adopt a model a long time before necessary to allow for discussion and understanding to develop. If you wait until your children are already involved with someone emotionally, it will be far more difficult to change the direction of the relationship. All three of our children married, and we actually had five courtship experiences. All five worked to varying degrees, and we learned a great deal through each of them.

Our firstborn was subjected to a very strict, narrow understanding of courtship. Her husband practically had to sign a document stating that he intended to marry our daughter before I would let him even meet her. It seems like many of us parents experiment on our firstborns, and I am sure there is a special reward in heaven for all of them.

The young man's father called me one day and asked if I would be willing to have lunch with him and his son. The son was away at college and could not find a girl that wanted to stay at home and be a mom. All the girls at college were very forward and not what he was interested in at all. His dad told him he knew of such a girl that might just work. We had a great lunch lasting about three hours and began the process of interviewing. I really did not know what I was doing, but I knew it was my job to "screen" out undesirable young men.

For months, Brian and I wrote back and forth, and I was able to get to know him at a deep level. I had always told my daughters to look for two qualities in a young man—teachableness and kindness. Good looks and muscles will fade, but these two traits will only get better as the years pass. Brian had both of them in abundance! Of course, he was not too bad looking either. Over the next year or so, they fell in love and married. We attempted to provide encouragement, supervision, and assistance as they entered into the engagement process.

In addition to looking for certain character qualities, such as teachableness and kindness, I encouraged my children to observe their prospective mate's interaction with his or her family. How does the young man or woman interact with his or her parents and siblings? Is he or she respectful or rebellious? Is he or she inclusive and loving with siblings or nasty and hateful? The parents are this person's family, and after you say, "I do" you become family as well. The way he or she treats family is a very good indication of how he or she will treat you after you become family. Choose wisely.

My son actually had two courtship experiences. The first one was with the daughter of a family that we had known for many years. They entered into the courtship to determine if marriage was what God had for them. After a period of time, it became clear that this was not God's will for either of them. While painful, the courtship was ended. Eventually the pain subsided, and both ended up marrying others who were more suitable. Even though the courtship did not end in marriage, the goal of the relationship was not simply pleasure oriented but an honest evaluation of marriage suitability.

My middle daughter also had two courtship experiences. One ended similarly to our son's, and the other resulted in an excellent marriage to a delightful young man. Sarah was twenty-eight when she married, and this waiting time provided her many opportunities to travel and serve before becoming a wife. As Sarah watched her older sister and younger brother marry, the natural questions were asked. "What is wrong with me? Why am I not married?" Our counsel to her was to follow Paul's instructions to singles in 1 Corinthians 7—be wholly devoted to the Lord and be concerned with investing in others while you wait.

Our daughter did this wonderfully, and we were extremely proud of her. It was not always easy, but she decided to spend her time serving. She travelled to China to teach and assist a missionary. She became a cosmetologist so she could provide a necessary service to families that didn't have a lot of money. And, as I previously mentioned, she invested in the young girls in our church. Sarah became "Auntie Sarah" to about forty young girls. These same girls were all invited to sing as a choir in her wedding when the day finally arrived. It was quite a sight and brought tears to just about everyone's eyes. Only God knows the eternal impact made by one older daughter being willing to invest in the lives of young girls!

Courtship is not a magic solution and is no guarantee that your children will not have struggles morally or that they will end in a successful marriage. As I mentioned in the first chapter, every child grows up and becomes an adult that is fully capable of making foolish, sinful decisions. Only Jesus is perfect, and only He lived a sinless life. Adult children can and do fall. As parents of adult children, we must be there to help them recover and pick up the pieces, as God supplies the grace.

We chose courtship over dating because my wife and I were products of the dating system. From our perspective, dating prepares a person for divorce, not marriage. The selfish, pleasure-seeking aspect of dating does not properly prepare someone for the death-to-self traits necessary for marriage. Spending time with someone and becoming emotionally and/or physically entangled with them, then simply walking away for another person, does not produce stability or the commitment necessary to survive in our world. Divorce is rampant in the church, and perhaps one reason is that we are following the world's method of casual partner swapping. Marriage is hard work and takes deep commitment in order to succeed.

Whatever method you choose to follow, parental involvement and of course moral purity should be the goal. Many marriage issues that require years of counseling to overcome begin during the pre-marriage relationship. Sexual exploration and experimentation, while pleasurable for the couple, often lead to long-term problems. Sexual sin is the one sin that we are told to run from (1 Corinthians 6:18), and the reason is obvious: it is extremely difficult to resist in the heat of the moment. One sure way to avoid sexual failure is to take along a younger sibling or never allow yourself to be in a place where you cannot be interrupted. Pulling off on a side road and getting into the backseat of a car will not help you avoid sexual failure unless your younger brother is back there!

Sometimes young people fall in love and press ahead in marrying their choice, regardless of parental cautions or objections. In regard to selection of a life partner for marriage, I have yet to meet anyone who did not sooner or later regret their decision to rebel against their parents, and if they could do it over again, they would not have done so. I have worked with hundreds of people who regret their foolish choice, and they wish they could go back and change it. Even if their marriage is successful, they live with a nagging regret that they did not have their parents' blessing on the union. Often though, their marriages are riddled with guilt and difficulties stemming from the pride and arrogance of not properly dealing with parents' objections. Many times, parents have God-given insight into the difficulties that the marriage will encounter, and any couple that is trying to follow the LORD will want their parents' blessing on that marriage. Pushing ahead without their parents' consent will dishonor the parents and make for a rocky foundation. The demanding of my own way, over the objections of the parents, also is a confession of unbelief. In essence, this action is stating that God is simply unable to change the parental authority to agree with your direction, so then you must take action. It is far better to pray and allow God to change your parents' (or your!) heart, than to press on with the marriage.

Choosing a life partner is a momentous decision. I have often stated, "It is far better to be happily married for forty years than to be miserably married for fifty." If it takes ten years to find the right mate, you will not regret the time spent in waiting.

QUESTIONS TO PRAY ABOUT

Have you been praying for your children's future spouses?

What do we consider to be the two most important qualities in a spouse for our children?

Are my children attracted to someone of the opposite sex?

Have we been discussing our goals regarding dating or courtship with our children?

Am I walking in moral purity daily?

Is my marriage something that I would want my children to imitate?

> "Children progressively understand what a parent and the wider church members love and appreciate. Year after year, their understanding builds. Year after year, the well is filling up. The cumulative effect of deep and significant thinking and activities is what we are looking for."
>
> —Scott Brown, director of The National Center for Family Integrated Churches–*Children in the Meeting of the Ephesian Church*

What about the Church?

So that through the church the manifold wisdom of God might
now be made known to the rulers and authorities in the heavenly
places.

Ephesians 3:10

The church can be one of the biggest dividers of the home, but it is
still God's plan and it is not to be forsaken. Jesus gave His life for the
church, and it is within this gathering of saints that our Christian
life is supposed to grow and flourish. It is in the church that we learn
how to walk in love and unity, and these two attributes will produce
power and a significant testimony to the reality of God. In the gathering of believers, we learn to worship, pray, and be instructed in the
Word of God. Forsaking it is simply not a good option.

And let us consider how to stir up one another to love and good
works not neglecting to meet together, as is the habit of some,
but encouraging one another, and all the more as you see the
Day drawing near.

Hebrews 10:24–25

However, the church needs to evaluate what she is doing and her
effectiveness in reaching the next generation. Much of what is done
under the heading of "church" is not biblically mandated. I firmly
believe we need to understand that the church should be comple-
menting, not competing with the family.

In many churches strong pressure is placed on already busy families to help carry out the vision of the church. There is nothing inherently wrong with a church having a vision. However, I believe the family, not the programs of the church, should be primary. The family unit is being destroyed, and the impact lasts for generations. If a church program fails, how long of an impact will it have? If an outreach has less than expected attendance or if a building addition does not get erected will generations be affected? However, a divorce suffered or a son or daughter lost will have a significantly greater impact than a failed program. Sadly, which one of these receives the greater attention via time and money from many churches?

I believe the first priority of the church should be to strengthen the family, not divide it. A typical church that is labeled a "family church" simply means that the family is divided into many age-segregated parts. One church in our city that proclaims that it is a family church has eighty-one ministries! The church has segregated to such an extent that in many churches there are multiple weekly meetings and staff required for every age group between newborns and the elderly. These staff positions often include children's church, junior church, youth church, senior high church, young singles, college and career, older singles, young married without kids, young married with kids, and senior citizens. In addition, churches routinely offer classes for every school-age group and for those married, based on age, as well as classes and events geared to the "senior saints."

Where are the classes for family-integration? What about classes or staff assigned to assist fathers in leading their homes or mothers in investing in the next generation? Perhaps classes should be offered on "how to lead family devotions and make a generational impact." What about adding pastors or staff who are in charge of "marriage stability"? Where is the staff member in charge of "divorce prevention" or "teenage rebellion avoidance"? In most churches, these are lacking or not even considered.

The vision to completely segregate the family and grow both the buildings and the staff is firmly in place in most evangelical churches. To even challenge these well-entrenched concepts places one outside of acceptability. We, as the church, need to wake up, because the young people are leaving the faith in droves as they enter college. Estimates range from 70–90 percent of our churched young people rejecting the faith in their first year of college! Our system of training them is failing miserably, yet we continue to repeat it with even greater emphasis. Churches add more staff and spend millions of dollars in children's and youth ministry, yet the results are dismal. It is time to think outside of this commonly held system of ministry.

The hard truth is that countless activities take the place of the family togetherness, and many parents are content to delegate their responsibility of training their children to the church staff. Youth pastors are barely older than the youth they are trying to lead. Many pastors have failed as parents and are not qualified to teach others how to raise their families. Ministry is substituted for parenting, and the Great Commission is used to heap guilt on parishioners in order to fulfill the pastor's vision.

I firmly believe the Scripture points to children being in church with their parents and that the parents should be the primary source of spiritual training for them. While others may complement what is taught, the parents are the ones held responsible for the teaching. Children will learn more valuable character traits by watching their parents worship, pray, and revere God's Word than they will ever learn from entertainment-oriented high-energy skits or cute puppets. I believe in the validity of the local church and that all believers should be ministered to, but I also believe our churches need to rethink what we are doing to the family unit. The family is being destroyed, and the church seems to be fiddling like Nero when Rome burned. We cannot continue on with business as usual, given the generational destruction taking place.

I recently finished my PhD dissertation with Trinity Seminary. My thesis explored the topic of the biblical role of the parents and the church in faith impartation to the next generation. During this research, it became obvious that I was encroaching on some very deep-rooted and sacred ideas. Using only Scripture, I built a case for the parents being *the* central figure in faith transference. There is not a single, clear example of age-segregation anywhere in either Testament but hundreds of age-integrated ones. The family is almost always presented as being together. Other than the "forty youths" that ended up being mauled by two bears, and the young associates of Solomon's son that gave very bad counsel, groups of young people are never mentioned. On the other hand, parents and children of all ages are together in almost every gathering recorded.

There is no age segregation in the Scripture. That statement caused me a significant amount of work and added months to the completion of my PhD research. I had the audacity to reveal the obvious, and sparks flew! My professors were trained in Christian education, youth, and children's ministry, and I dared to state that these are not biblically based methods of reaching the next generation. In fact, I went so far as to state that these methods are failing in huge numbers as revealed by many studies. For the record, I do not fault my professors; they were simply walking out what they had been taught.

The only group not experiencing these levels of failure are those that home educated their children. This group is enjoying an inverse success rate of faith impartation! Current studies reveal that over 90 percent of home-educated adults still significantly agree with and maintain their parents' faith! Those raised in the typical age-segregated environment are leaving their parents' faith in huge numbers, thus pointing to the conclusion that those who spent the majority of their time with their parents are keeping their faith!

Why won't the majority of the churches adopt some sort of age-integration ministry given the dismal results being gained in the commonly accepted one? The answer is not a simple one. First, almost every seminary and Bible college promotes the age-segregated approach to ministry. Pastors are told that in order to build a successful church, you have to minister to the children and youth. Ask any children or youth worker, and they will tell you that there is a significantly better chance of someone accepting Christ before the age of eighteen than afterwards. So time and money is invested in order to reach the children before they reach adulthood. I agree with the reality of children being easier to reach with the gospel, but I disagree with *who* is primarily responsible to do the reaching! I believe it should be the parents, not the organized church, doing the reaching and the discipling of the children.

Next, pastors are told that the parents need a break away from the children in order to hear the message undistracted, so the church has to provide nurseries and an excellent children's ministry. However, many parents end up "serving" in these ministries and miss the message anyway. In addition, many parents have already spent huge blocks of time away from their children during the week. Fathers and mothers often work outside of the home and the children go to school, so there has been significant time spent away from each other. Many families participate in sports and other events, which sometimes require a major commitment of time and family segregation.

From my point of view, we are doing the children and the parents a disservice by providing these "babysitting" services. We are alleviating the parents of their God-given mandate to teach their children, and we are training the children that "big" church is boring. We take babies and give them toys, crackers, and juice as distractions instead of training them to sit quietly with their parents. Toddlers up through preteens are isolated away from the adults and entertained with puppets, skits, and loud, quick-moving videos. Teens are often given pabulum instead of meat in junior church, and when they reach some magical age, they are thrust into "real" church. And we wonder why they are all bored!

The parents have been cheated out of being the primary teacher to their children, and the fathers have missed an opportunity to be considered wise as they answered the children's questions after the service. What a shame. In addition, the children are deprived of learning how important God's Word is by observing their parents' attentiveness during the service. How much better it would be if the children could be brought back into the service, as was always the case in Scripture. Until recent history (1970s), the family remained intact on Sundays, listening to the pastor and then discussing what was taught over the afternoon meal.

It would be easy to blame the organized church for all of the problems, but truthfully the primary blame rests right where it should—on the parents. The vast majority of parents are delighted that the church offers babysitting and teaching for their children. The delegation of this responsibility to the church is a welcome relief to many parents. *Now my children will have excellent training and instruction by professionals*, goes the thinking. *The children and youth workers are trained, and they will do a much better job than I would*, thinks the parent. Having been a pastor for thirty years, I would beg to disagree. Most of the workers are fellow parents or young people who simply are not trained. Those who are trained are educated in a system that is producing a 70–90 percent failure rate. The painful reality is that it is easy to delegate the spiritual training of the children away because with that delegation comes some insulation later on. "It is not my fault when my teen rejects my faith; I did everything I could to give them the best education possible! I sent them to Sunday school, children's church, youth group, and Christian school. What more could I have possibly done?"

What parents should do, and the church ought to insist that they really do it, is train their own children. Parents must take the primary role in this process. Fathers need to be leading their children daily and not just leaving it to the professionals. The parents must be the primary role models for the next generation, and that position cannot be delegated to anyone else. Rather than dividing the family into parts, the church should be strengthening all of the family together, thus helping to solidify the core of our society by offering to help fathers and mothers in these areas. Pastors should be reinforcing with their sermons what the parents are teaching at home and vice versa. If we keep doing the same things that we have been doing, I believe we will keep getting the same results. It is time to rethink church before it is too late.

HOW DOES A FAMILY-INTEGRATED CHURCH WORK?

One unique distinctive of the family-integrated churches is that the family is not segregated as soon as the family enters the building. The family is encouraged to experience the church service and most activities together. Children sit with the parents during the entire worship service; therefore nurseries, children's ministries, and youth specific services are not part of church life. Parents are encouraged to be the peer group of their children, and fathers are challenged to take the responsibility to lead and train their family. Specific teaching and training is directed to fathers and mothers to help them fulfill their biblical roles, and the church resists interfering or subverting those roles. Parents are expected to fulfill the role of the youth, children's, and singles' pastor and not delegate this task back to the church. Doug Phillips sums it up well:

> I have the privilege of worshiping in a small, family-integrated church. When asked about our various church programs, I explain that we are blessed with more than thirty different organizations to which our members belong—they are called families. I further explain that we have more than sixty youth directors—they are called parents. In fact, we have such a full schedule of events that there is a mandatory activity every day of the week—it is called family worship.
> —Doug Phillips, Esq., "Our Church Youth Group"

THE ROLE OF THE PASTOR

A philosophical shift as to the role of the pastor(s) occurs between the departmental, age-segregated model and the family-integrated one. Often in a departmental model, the congregation is encouraged to participate in the life of the church via activities and events, typically centered in the pastor or staff. For example, "the youth group will be taking a trip to Mexico" might be advertised in a church bulletin. On this trip the sponsoring church would provide leadership and staff, etc. Alternatively, there may be any number of causes, events, or programs that the church would want to emphasize, and they will usually provide staff to bring supervision and coordination for the event. Typical promotions will begin with, "Come join us as we ... "

In a family-integrated model, families *still* go on a mission trip to Mexico, and the pastor may or may not participate. The church might not even be involved. If asked, the church could assist with prayer, help make connections or assist with cash, but the initiative is parent driven, not staff driven. The focus is on what the family wants to do to provide an outreach for their children, not what the church wants to do to mobilize people. The same would be true for nursing home ministry, pro-life work, evangelism, children and youth ministry. The family is centric, not the church building or pastor. While this may seem unorthodox, the apostle Paul stated one of the jobs of the pastor was to "equip the saints to do the work of the ministry" in Ephesians 4:11–12. In the traditional age-segregated, departmental church, *equip* often means we do, and you join us. In the family-integrated church equip means, you do, and we (church leadership) train and support.

Under this ministry model, the pastor's role changes from activity director and program initiator, to one that teaches the people how to do whatever ministry they are being led by God to perform. The pastor's job is to train the people through the teaching of the Scripture. The pastor explains to the people how to live a Christian life every day in the home, at school, and at the workplace. The philosophical mind-set could be summed up in this statement: "ministry is birthed out of a functioning home." A home that is functioning according to biblical principles will produce evangelism, outreach to the neighborhood, hospitality, missions, and a host of other service projects. From the home, families can conduct evangelism in their neighborhood, sing and teach at nursing homes, work in pro-life counseling, take positions in the schools to support teachers, administration, and students, go to foreign countries to serve, work in food pantries, conduct small groups in their home, etc. All of these require little (budget or time wise) from the church or pastor and are family driven in obedience to God's leading. The pastor trains, encourages, and releases. When the parents believe that their family is ready to serve, they serve as God directs. This does not mean that the pastor or church never does anything, but the *primary* responsibility for ministry comes from the home, not the organized church or its leadership. When the church leadership believes that their church should do something, the opportunities are presented with the emphasis being placed on whether this is a fit for each individual family. No pressure is brought for every member to participate, but outreaches and events are available for those that care to participate. This reinforces the role of the parents as the leaders and initiators of their families ministry endeavors.

THE TYPICAL AGE-INTEGRATED CHURCH SERVICE

A typical church service of a family-integrated church would not be very different from a family-segregated one. The primary difference would be *who* is in the service. The children remain with their parents and are not isolated into groupings with their peers. Scott Brown, the director of the National Center for Family-Integrated Churches, comments as follows on Ephesians 6:

> "In the first two verses, Paul is clearly speaking to children. These are the children who are in the meeting of the Ephesian church and are hearing the letter read. Paul uses a Greek grammatical form called the vocative case, called the "vocative of direct address." He is directly addressing the children in the meeting of the church. This makes it an obvious fact that children were present in the meetings of the early churches."
> —"Children in the Meeting of the Ephesian Church"

Some might argue that the children are not receiving any benefit from the teaching because they do not understand all of the words being spoken. I would strongly disagree. The children are observing their parents and older siblings if they have them, and this observation can speak volumes. I believe that the child can learn the importance of worship as they observe their parents worship. The child can learn to respect the Word of God as they observe their parents' attentiveness to the teaching. The child can learn the importance of sitting quietly so others can listen. The child can learn the value of being together even if it is not entertaining or pleasurable. The child can learn that there are more important issues than simply their personal entertainment.

In reality, children do listen to what is being sung and taught. If they can understand words, they often will ask their parents about them as they think about them later. Many conversation opportunities take place as young children ask questions about something they either sang or heard during the service. This allows the father or mother to enter into a teaching mode with the children. These conversations allow adult-level discussions to take place, which will help the child mature and develop mentally. These questions asked will also force the parents to be better prepared to answer them, thus helping to cement the pastor's message further into the mind of the parents. When children are isolated from the adults and taught by puppets or others at a very young level, it hinders the parents from having the opportunity to be the child's teacher and mentor. Many parents in the family-integrated churches will encourage their children to listen for specific words during the sermon and to write them down. Words like *faith* or *joy* can easily be written and then discussed later with the children to assure they understand what was taught.

A final comment from Brown's article sums up the heart cry of many within the family-integrated model and notice that the family of faith is still important:

> We enjoy eating out together as a family. We enjoy going to the beach together as a family. Then, why do we not enjoy worship and instruction and fellowship as a family with our spiritual family of brothers and sisters?

In the family-integrated model, relationships take precedence over programs and activities. Beyond the goal of strengthening the family relationships between parents and children, the marital relationship is valued and emphasized as central. When a marriage is falling apart through divorce or simply reduced to a truce, rather than oneness that the Scripture calls for in Ephesians 5, the gospel is hindered from going forth. A functioning home where both father and mother love each other is critical for evangelism, outreach, and a multigenerational impact. When the home falls apart, it has devastating results, not only in the home, but also in the kingdom of God. Thus, significant teaching and efforts will be invested in the family-integrated model to assist marriages through teaching, counseling, modeling, and mentoring.

Older children are encouraged to invest in the lives of younger children, thus promoting an inter-generational impact. The importance of an eighteen-year-old talking to and befriending an eleven-year-old can only be appreciated by remembering how we would have loved for it to happen to us when we were eleven. Integrating the ages from birth to grandparents can positively affect both the young and old. The potential for wisdom transference from older to younger is immense when everyone is comfortable with interacting. When each age is isolated to their own assemblage, it becomes increasingly difficult to find common ground or interest with those outside of your grouping. In the departmental, age-segregated model, it is unusual to observe the intergenerational interaction that is common in the family-integrated model.

In addition to the typical objection of children not being able to understand the sermon, other issues often arise when considering the practical aspects of family-integrated ministry. The noise issue of children being in church is an example. Many pastors and adults simply do not want to deal with noisy children since they can be a distraction. In the family-integrated model, parents are encouraged to train their children to sit quietly during the service. This training typically takes place at home during the week. Children often sit for hours watching TV or coloring, so it is not the lack of ability to sit quietly but the lack of training on the parents' part to expect it from the children. Many family-integrated churches will offer a cry room or a place for parents to take their babies or toddlers to help them learn to become quiet. After the baby or child quiets down, the parents are encouraged to reenter the service and continue the training process. Most children can learn to sit still if the parents will train them. Of course, there are special needs children or undisciplined children that will need additional help and support. In the family-integrated church, often this is an opportunity for older children to assist another family by helping with the child, thus reinforcing the intergenerational goal.

HOW IS IT WORKING IN REALITY?

At Hope Family Fellowship a great deal of ministry takes place that the pastors are not involved in or responsible for directing. Some of the ones that I am aware of include outreaches to the poor providing free clothing, hospital visitation, nursing home ministry, jail outreaches, service at economically challenged youth centers, men's and women's meetings, various home group Bible studies, neighborhood outreaches, foreign mission trips, service projects to assist several parachurch organizations, providing handmade hats and quilts for premature babies at two hospitals, providing gifts for inmates' children and families, marriage counseling, academic tutoring, summer camp counseling, and the list could go on for quite a while. The point is that the families will learn to minister where they live and not be tied to a staff person's vision. My job as a pastor is to assist and equip as needed to release people into effective working for the kingdom of God. Since the pastor or staff is not tied up with the details of providing ministry outlets for the families, more time can be devoted to study, prayer, and actually interacting with the people.

While family-integrated ministry would seem to limit outreach and mission, the exact opposite is occurring. The natural outworking of a functioning home is outreach. A home in chaos has little to offer a hurting world. Where marriages are struggling to survive, and where children do not like their parents or each other, little of value can be exported. Where marriages are healthy and growing in oneness and where the parent child relationship is one of partnership, not adversarial, the normal result will be outreach and a desire to serve others. Thus, the family-integrated model's primary emphasis is placed on strengthening and encouraging the family as a whole and not focusing on its individual components.

At Hope Family Fellowship an age-integrated worship team leads the congregation in a time of worship, thus helping to reinforce the overall vision. Young people are part of the service and are not considered the church of the future but the church of today. In fact, age integration takes place at most activities, even gender-specific ones. Hope Family Fellowship has men's and women's gatherings that are open to all ages. There are home fellowships and studies, service opportunities, mission trips, prayer meetings, and other gatherings that are all open to the entire family. Hope encourages the inter-generational interaction as part of our vision, older men and women helping the younger ones by sharing their victories as well as failures. Singles and those that have suffered through a divorce are incorporated into the bigger family of the church. Why isolate everyone away from each other when there is so much to share? It seems so much wiser to share the accumulated wisdom so the next generation does not have to completely relearn what the older ones already know.

There is no such thing as a perfect church, and Hope Family Fellowship fits into that statement. People are involved; therefore problems exist. Perfection or being exclusive is not the goal but to make sure that parents are doing everything they can to invest in and capture the next generation for Christ. While the age-segregated church model continues to experience 70–90 percent of their children walking away from the faith as they enter college or the workforce, early studies and testimonies show that the family-integrated church model is far exceeding this dismal return on the churches investment.

So, the next time you are at a church service, please prayerfully consider keeping your children with you. The benefits of this decision far outweigh any perceived loss you or they may believe will incur. By being with you, your children will be allowed to hear the same message you are hearing. They will observe you as you follow along in the Scripture, take notes, and worship your God. When they encounter material that they don't understand, then you get the blessing of being the instructor, thus raising their opinion of you. The joyful result with be that unity will increase in your home as you share the same experiences.

QUESTIONS TO PRAY ABOUT

Have I given up on the church and the assembling together with other believers?

Am I involved so deeply in church activities that my family time is suffering?

Have I embraced a nonbiblical view of family segregation?

Have I attempted to delegate away my responsibility to train my own children to the organized church?

Am I willing to pray about keeping my children with me and teaching them myself?

> "The church should be known as a place where God is worshiped, where the Word of God is heard and practiced, and where life is thought about and given its most searching and serious analysis...Today, the interest turns to how well appointed and organized the church is, what programs it has to offer, how many outings the youth group has organized, how convenient it is to attend, how good the nursery is."
>
> —David Wells, professor at Gordon-Conwell Theological Seminary quoted from *No Place For Truth*

A Note to Grandparents

Grandchildren are the crown of the aged, and the glory of children is their fathers.

Proverbs 17:6

When our first granddaughter arrived, there was an instant bonding between us, at least from my point of view. I held her in my arms, and delight filled my heart as I gazed at that little girl. I marveled and rejoiced that I had lived to see this day. At age forty-two, it was quite a jolt to be a grandfather, but it was a delightful shock! When Lydia arrived, my wife and I needed to evaluate our roles as grandparents. We were not her parents, yet there seemed to be something we were supposed to be doing beyond what the bumper stickers proclaimed about grandchildren (spoiling them and sending them home or spending their inheritance). There certainly was a strong generational connection, but we were not sure what our responsibilities were.

Those of us who have given our lives to the raising of our children can find our new roles as grandparents somewhat confusing. As parents, we exercised almost complete control over our children until they were adults. Eating, sleeping, education, clothing, and just about every other decision was made on behalf of the child, or at least in concert with them. As our children grew, we were very involved right up until they left our home. Now, here is a newborn baby, and the temptation is to resume our former roles. However, this must be resisted! These little ones are not ours but belong to other parents who are just beginning the task we have completed. So what are we supposed to do as grandparents?

Here are a few lessons we have learned on our grandparent journey so far. First, pray often for the new parents. They need wisdom and insight on how to adjust to the new family member, and they will need an abundance of guidance as the child grows. Second, be available to assist in babysitting, house cleaning, cooking, and any practical matter needed. Like so many, it would have been wonderful to have a night out now and again when our children were young. We simply did not have that option. Now we can provide that for our grown children, and they have all told us that it is such a blessing! Third, always remember to turn the heart of the child back to the parents. These precious gifts are not yours but belong to their parents. Our job as grandparents is to reinforce what the parents want, not to contradict or undermine. Sometimes this can be challenging, because by the time we become grandparents we certainly have learned a few things from our experiences. We observe the mistakes of youth, and the temptation is to jump in and give an unsolicited opinion. A proverb I coined years ago goes like this:

> Woe to the man who gives his opinion when it is not being asked; it will be reckoned unto him as a curse!

If we develop a trusting relationship with our children as they age, our opinions will be asked for and valued when they are older and in need of our assistance. However, giving our opinion to our adult children before it is requested can result in being labeled as a meddler, can cause resentment, and can potentially damage your relationship for years.

One key point is that we must never undermine the parents to the grandchildren even if we disagree with the parents. If we observe harmful or dangerous behavior, then we must appeal to the parents discreetly, but never turn the hearts of the children away from their parents. We must reinforce what the parents are doing, not undercut it. Remember what you wish your parents had done when you had your children still at home … then try to be that person! When a grandchild asks us for anything, if the parents are around, we always send them back to the parents, thus keeping the lines of authority clear. Grandparents that sneak behind the parents' backs are teaching rebellion and disrespect for authority, so we must be careful what we teach by our actions and attitudes!

As grandparents, we are modeling to another generation (whether we realize it or not) what it looks like to walk with God. Self-focused grandparents are missing a great opportunity to invest in the future. Our culture glorifies self-gratification, and unfortunately, many godly people have bought into this lifestyle without considering the outcome of this choice. The thought goes something like this—"I have lived my whole life raising my children. Now I'm going to enjoy life and take care of me!" This lifestyle is evidenced by multitudes of grandparents moving to the coasts or deserts instead of staying by their families. From my perspective, this is a waste of experience and a loss to the next generation. Someone said years ago that very few people in nursing homes regret not spending more time at the office or on vacation, but almost all regret the time lost with their families. We never get to spend time twice, so we must choose wisely the first time!

Even if you feel you have nothing to offer because your life has been full of mistakes, you have your love and experience to offer. One of the best ways to gain knowledge is by learning from other people's mistakes and then trying to avoid repeating them. How beneficial it would be for the older generation to pass on to the younger one the wisdom that was learned from all those mistakes. Do not waste them by keeping them all to yourself! Experiences, both good and bad, should be passed on to those who follow us, for each event possesses a lesson or insight.

As grandparents, our goal should be to be godly examples who love and serve the next generation. We need to avoid violating the parents' authority and instead reinforce it to their children. We are not called to spoil grandchildren but to help in the training process of them. We are blessed to enjoy this gift from God and take our responsibilities seriously and not simply live to gratify our flesh.

Another generation is at stake, and we must give ourselves selflessly to assist in capturing it for Christ!

I appeal to the grandparents (and future ones) to consider their involvement with the next generation. Is warmer weather really worth missing this opportunity? Playing golf and having abundant free time is great, but what about investing in your grandchildren or great grandchildren? What about taking time to share your story with them? I love the ocean and taking walks where I enjoy breath-taking views, but I would rather not ever see them again than miss my grandchildren's lives! I can visit the ocean, but moving away from my family is not an option. I would rather shovel ten feet of snow than miss the fellowship and joy of my children and grandchildren. Wouldn't you? Your family needs you more than the RV park or your bunko partners do.

What could you do to help? How about offering to homeschool the child or children one day a week for the frazzled mom? Perhaps babysitting once in a while to allow the parents a night out for plea-sure or even some necessary shopping. Please consider writing out your personal testimony for the next generation, sharing some of your success stories or failures, focusing on what you learned from them. We all have so much to offer—may we not waste our knowl-edge! Please prayerfully consider where and how you live out the rest of your days. It is not too late to reengage in the battle, for the next generation is at stake!

QUESTIONS TO PRAY ABOUT

Have I been supportive of my children in their role as parents?

Have I tried to turn the heart of the grandchildren back to the parents?

Do I have a servant's heart, or am I self-centered concerning my children?

When we are together, do my grandchildren see a godly example or something less when they observe my life?

If I have chosen to live somewhere away from my family, does God wants me to reconsider it?

> "The happiest moments of my life have been the few which I have passed at home in the bosom of my family."
>
> —Thomas Jefferson

SOME FINAL THOUGHTS

A desire fulfilled is sweet to the soul.

Proverbs 13:19a

Successful parenting will produce the greatest joy in your life, more than any job, ministry, money, or any other success. When we die, we will give an account for what we have done with what we have been given. All of us have been given gifts from our Creator, including life and a family. What have we done with them? It is sometimes stated that we take nothing out of this life, and to a point, this is true. However, if we really are laying up treasure in heaven, and if we are going to give an account to our God with what we have done with the "talents" we have been given, then that thought is not quite true. God has entrusted us with our families, and He expects us to do something of value with them. What a gift, and it is quite the challenge!

If you believe that you have been a failure up to this point, take courage! We all fail, and the Scripture offers great hope in this area.

For the righteous falls seven times and rises again, but the wicked stumble in times of calamity.

Proverbs 24:16

If we confess our sins, he is faithful and just to forgive us our sins and to cleanse us from all unrighteousness.

1 John 1:9

> Let us then with confidence draw near to the throne of grace, that we may receive mercy and find grace to help in time of need.
>
> Hebrews 4:16

When we fall, and we all fall, we must fall in the right direction—toward the LORD and heading toward the pathway of holiness. We can get back up because God gives us the strength to go on and to keep on walking with Him. When we sin, we can go to the throne and find mercy, grace, and forgiveness from the King of kings and LORD of lords. Failure is not an excuse for quitting. Failure is a reason to approach God for grace and receive the necessary tools to proceed. God has given us a task, and we must press on in His strength. We can learn from our mistakes, explain them to our children, and use them as an example not to be repeated. We may fail, but we are not failures! We are children of the King, and He will give us what we need to be successful if we will but ask Him.

If your children are already grown and you now recognize some past failures, then go to them, humble yourself, and ask for forgiveness. If you are reading this and your children are still at home, you probably have time to make the changes necessary to still be successful. Ruthlessly evaluate your life and cut out anything that is unnecessary and is stealing from what really matters. Move; change jobs, churches, or cities; but do whatever it takes to make the changes. Your family is worth whatever the price tag of change. If you are willing to make the changes, you will enjoy the fruit of your labors, and the truth of the Scripture will come alive. There really is "no greater joy," and children are a "rich reward" and a "heritage." You are blessed if "your quiver is full." Do not let another day go by without making a change in the right direction. Complete, drastic changes do not happen overnight, but changes will never happen if you do nothing. Pray, cry out to God, and make the changes necessary to impact the next generation.

Thank you for spending some time reading my thoughts. If there are ideas in this book that are helpful, then please feel free to use them. If you can't agree with everything written, then put into place what you can. Our families need us and a lost, and dying world is waiting for someone to demonstrate that strong, united, loving families are possible and that they really do make a difference worth living for—will you be one?

QUESTIONS TO PRAY ABOUT

Am I willing to evaluate every area of my life and see what changes need to take place? If not, why not?

Do I need to seek out my spouse or child(ren) and ask for forgiveness for something?

Have I been living in guilt when freedom is available?

Will I change as the LORD directs?

> "Jesus' presence in the family comes to its sharpest focus as the family gathers in His presence to worship. For worship is communion with God par excellence. In worship we gather in His presence; we assemble under His Lordship; we reach out to receive His grace; we listen to His Word; we submit ourselves to His will."
>
> —Larry Christenson quoted from *The Christian Family*

APPENDIX

SUGGESTED READINGS

What the Bible Says About Child Training—Richard Fugate
The Other Side of the Garden—Virginia Fugate
Discovering the Mind of a Woman—Ken Nair
Point Man and *Finishing Strong*—both books by Steve Farrah
Courage to Flee—Dr. Jeffrey A. Klick
The Family Integrated Church—Mark Fox

SOME SUGGESTED BOOKS TO READ ALOUD

Pilgrim's Progress—John Bunyan
Hinds Feet on High Places—Hannah Hurnard
Mountains of Spice—Hannah Hurnard
Tales of the Resistance—David and Karen Mains
Christian Mother Goose—Marjorie Decker

LIVE

listen|imagine|view|experience

AUDIO BOOK DOWNLOAD INCLUDED WITH THIS BOOK!

In your hands you hold a complete digital entertainment package. In addition to the paper version, you receive a free download of the audio version of this book. Simply use the code listed below when visiting our website. Once downloaded to your computer, you can listen to the book through your computer's speakers, burn it to an audio CD or save the file to your portable music device (such as Apple's popular iPod) and listen on the go!

How to get your free audio book digital download:

1. Visit www.tatepublishing.com and click on the e|LIVE logo on the home page.
2. Enter the following coupon code:
   5b7e-d9d9-6861-6c3a-98ee-6d49-6547-7530
3. Download the audio book from your e|LIVE digital locker and begin enjoying your new digital entertainment package today!